PREACHING FROM SAMUEL

PREACHING

FROM

SAMUEL

ANDREW W. BLACKWOOD
Professor of Homiletics
THE THEOLOGICAL SEMINARY
Princeton, New Jersey

*The hope of a broken world is to find men
big enough to mend it.*   —JOHN BUCHAN

BAKER BOOK HOUSE
Grand Rapids, Michigan

© 1946 by Stone & Pierce

Paperback Edition
issued July 1975 by
Baker Book House
with permission of copyright owner

ISBN: 0-8010-0641-4

PHOTOLITHOPRINTED BY CUSHING - MALLOY, INC.
ANN ARBOR, MICHIGAN, UNITED STATES OF AMERICA
1975

FOREWORD

THIS BOOK HAS GROWN OUT OF "PREACHING FROM THE BIBLE." THAT
volume dealt with various parts of the Scriptures and with
different kinds of pulpit work. This work has to do with a single
portion of Holy Writ and with one kind of preaching material.
In the two books alike the stress falls on practical uses of biblical
material, not on matters of technical scholarship. Such matters
have their place, as I discovered when I taught the Old Testament,
beginning with the Hebrew. In more recent years I have been
trying to show men how to use in the pulpit the findings of biblical study. This is the project now before us.

The project calls for singling out a definite field in the
Scriptures, and for working intensively. The choice of the book
should depend on the interests of the pastor, and on the needs of
the congregation. Today we all feel concerned about the rebuilding of nations after World War II. As long as any present-day
clergyman lives he will have to contend with the aftereffects of
that global strife. Without harping on "this war-torn world" or
other outworn words, the parish interpreter must deal with the
aftermath of blood and tears as it affects his friend in the pew.
From this point of view, which is pastoral, to which part of the
Bible shall the minister turn?

The twin books of Samuel lend themselves admirably to such
use. No other portion of Holy Writ contains such a wealth and
variety of preaching materials for days of reconstruction. On
almost every page of First and Second Samuel striking characters
appear in action. Again and again the clash of mighty personalities

5

creates a feeling of suspense. That in turn leads to many an exciting climax. Without appearing theatrical, the narrative often becomes dramatic, even thrilling. That may be why it led to a course of expository "lectures" by the prince of English-speaking interpreters, Frederick W. Robertson. In 1848 he strove to meet his age's problems of rebuilding after war. Unfortunately, his discourses on Samuel are not available. But he has left an account of their origin.

When Robertson had just passed his thirty-fourth birthday he wrote as follows:

We began two years ago the practice of giving the Sunday morning to a sermon, and the afternoon to a lecture. The difference between the two was that in the morning we took for our subject a single text, and endeavoured to exhaust that; but in the afternoon a chapter, and endeavoured to expound the general truths contained therein. The sermon was hortatory and practical; the lecture was didactic. The first appealed to the heart and the conscience; the second rather to the intellect and the analytic faculty. In this way we have already considered in a series the Books of Samuel and the Acts of the Apostles. The book for exposition during the ensuing year is Genesis.[1]

During the period before his untimely death in 1853 the young interpreter also lectured on First and Second Corinthians.[2]

Why should not many a local minister preach from the Bible in these two ways? For a different fashion of doing much the same things, turn to the writings of Alexander Maclaren. In his published sermons he dealt with single texts, most of which were short and crisp. In the *Expositions* he singled out large units. Whatever the method employed, the young interpreter will find expository work difficult, especially at first. He could easily give a

---

[1] *Notes on Genesis* (London, 1886), p. 1.

[2] See his *Sermons on St. Paul's Epistles to the Corinthians*, Ticknor and Fields, 1868.

verse-by-verse monologue on an extended passage, but why refer to that as preaching? Such half-baked stuff is worth little more than it costs, which may be next to nothing. If the young minister is to follow in the footsteps of Robertson and Maclaren, however, there must be toil in the workshop, day after day.

The pages that follow open up all sorts of "leads" into fertile ground ready for the preacher. The first half of my book deals in detail with seventeen consecutive chapters in First Samuel, with the Bible paragraph serving as the unit of study. The latter half of the volume throws more stress on preaching values and not so much on exposition. After the middle of the book I assume that the reader can serve as his own interpreter. Since the limits of space do not allow me to discuss every passage in First and Second Samuel, I single out chapters that touch upon vital issues of today and tomorrow. For various reasons, I believe that the latter part of my book will prove the more interesting and rewarding. If so, the value will depend in part on what has gone before.

As a teacher of the most difficult art in all our world I hail with joy the increasing concern for sturdy sermon structure as well as beauty of style. Still I believe that every message from the Book should grow according to the life in the seed-thought of the sermon, and that the form of every sermon should depend on the personality of the minister and the needs of his friends in the pews. Hence I have not attempted to put these materials into finished homiletical form. I have simply tried to uncover the available preaching metal, from the purest gold to the crudest iron. I wish the reader to use the findings in many ways, including expository lectures and prayer meeting talks, "occasional" addresses at baccalaureate services, and popular biographical sermons. In any one case the use will depend on his program for the year's preaching.[8]

For help in preparing this volume I am grateful to countless

[8] See Blackwood, *Planning a Year's Pulpit Work*, Abingdon-Cokesbury, 1942.

students, here and elsewhere, and to many pastors near and far. Without such assistance I could never have subjected all these materials to searching laboratory tests. Unfortunately, I have found little of value in the available literature about the books of Samuel, and about expository preaching. In this respect, at least, my experience resembles that of F. W. Robertson. He relied mainly on the material he found in First and Second Samuel.

May the mantle of Robertson fall on many a reader. May the local parish minister find in First and Second Samuel an abundance of materials for preaching to the needs of today and tomorrow. Gradually he will begin to regard himself as the key man in the work of God's Kingdom. May he likewise claim the promise that the Holy Spirit shall shine upon the open page and bring the needed truth to light. Thus the local pastor will become a gifted interpreter of God's Holy Book.

ANDREW WATTERSON BLACKWOOD

CONTENTS

Part Three

THE MAN WHO LEADS IN REBUILDING

SECOND SAMUEL, CHAPTERS 1-24

LEADERS IN REBUILDING GOD'S NATION

THE TWO BOOKS OF SAMUEL BELONG TOGETHER AS ONE. THUS THEY appear in the original Hebrew Bible, where all the material was copied on a single scroll. But when the translators prepared the Septuagint, the Greek version of the Old Testament, they had to use two scrolls for this book. Hence it began to be known as First and Second Samuel. Really the two are as inseparable as Siamese twins.

The author of the twin books could not have been the prophet Samuel. IIis death is recorded before the twofold record is half complete.[1] However, his personality dominates the first half; and the two men whom he anointed for the kingship fill out most of the remainder. So the twin books are the lengthened shadow of the prophet whose name they bear, a man who in terms of today seems to have been much like a pastor.

The main portion of the twofold record appears to have come from an eye witness. The most likely candidates for the honor seem to be Ahimaaz and Abiathar.[2] According to a recent scholarly work the signs favor Ahimaaz. Concerning the un-identified author, Robert H. Pfeiffer, present-day interpreter of the Old Testament, speaks glowingly: "Whoever wrote the early source in Samuel is 'the father of history' in a much truer sense than Herodotus. . . . As far as we know, he created history as an

[1] I Sam. 25:1.
[2] See II Sam. 15:27, 36; 18:19-30; I Sam. 22:20-23; II Sam. 15:24, 29, 35-36; 17:15; 19:11; Mark 2:26.

11

art, as a recital of past events dominated by a great idea. . . . Without any previous models as guide, he wrote a masterpiece, unsurpassed in historicity, psychological insight, literary style, and dramatic power. . . . The style of the early source of Samuel (notably in II Sam. 9–20) is unsurpassed in the whole range of Hebrew prose literature."[3] Professor Pfeiffer quotes with approval a tribute to the ancient writer's mastery of prose, "which for combined simplicity and distinction has remained unmatched in the literature of the world, and which the progressive sophistication of mankind has long since rendered forever unapproachable."[4] But he does not highly esteem the portions of the Hebrew book that exalt David.

These critical matters interest us more than a little, but they do not seriously affect the preaching values of our twofold book. Some person must have been responsible for Samuel in its present form. Whatever his name and time in history, he has left a series of records that we find "profitable for teaching, for reproof, for correction, for instruction which is in righteousness."[5]

The two parts of Samuel deal with a period of nation-wide rebuilding. Chronologically, the narrative begins with the chaotic conditions that succeeded the era of the Judges. Then the course of events leads up to the so-called "golden age," about which we learn in First and Second Kings. These historical narratives, which come between Judges and Kings, bring before us three striking personalities: Samuel, Saul, and David. The part that most directly concerns Samuel closes with chapter 8 of First Samuel. For practical reasons, however, we shall treat the first twelve chapters as a unit. Thus we shall consider, in succession,

---

[3] *Introduction to the Old Testament* (Harper, 1941), pp. 357-59. The books of Samuel are treated on pp. 338-73.

[4] *Ibid.*, p. 359.

[5] II Tim. 3:16.

the pastor who guides in rebuilding, the ruler who fails in rebuilding, and the man who leads in rebuilding.

In order to master the twin books of Samuel the parish minister needs to map out a fairly extensive course of study at home. Ideally he would begin with the original Hebrew, and then work slowly. The present writer has done that in many parts of the twofold record. At one time he went rapidly through First Samuel in the Hebrew and the Greek, the Latin and the French, as well as the German. In the coming pages he will refer mainly to the American Revised Version, partly because of the division into paragraphs. He regrets that he has not had access to the forthcoming revision by present-day American scholars. That work should prove worthy of note for accuracy of translation and beauty of English prose.

For the bare facts about the books of Samuel turn to an up-to-date Bible dictionary.[6] For a critical account, study with care the above-mentioned work by Professor Pfeiffer. Then read the two books of Samuel as a whole, more than once, until the framework stands out in the mind's eye as a single unit. After that go through the record by paragraphs and put down on paper the gist of each successive portion. Give some heed, also, to the chapter divisions, or clusters of related paragraphs. On points of difficulty consult a popular commentary, such as the *New Century Bible*. Then ask some competent interpreter of the Old Testament to prepare a more adequate treatment of these books than our libraries now afford!

All the while keep the gaze fixed upon one of the three main characters, noting how divine Providence overrules his mistakes and failures. Gradually you will begin to see all sorts of preaching values. Many of them appear in this volume. Others do not, as the limits of space forbid an exhaustive treatment. Facility

---

[6] Such as John D. Davis, *The Westminster Dictionary of the Bible*, rev. and rewritten by Henry S. Gehman, Westminster, 1944.

in this way of approaching the Scriptures grows with daily use of a man's intellectual muscles. Above all, the interpreter of the Book must learn to *see*. For this reason a seminary professor uses concerning student after student the words of the Hebrew prophet: "Lord, I pray thee, open his eyes, that he may see." [7]

Years ago a young clergyman followed this kind of self-directed study at home. After almost a year of intensive work he became well acquainted with the books of Samuel. Then the young minister became a college president. From that time onward he never found time to master any other portion of the Old Testament. In later years he told pastoral friends that his careful study of these twin books had provided him with more preaching materials than he had been able to find in all the remainder of the Old Testament. Needless to say, a diligent parish minister will learn as much as possible about every major book in the Hebrew Bible. Even so, he will profit most from an intensive study of one book at a time. Why should any educated minister attempt to play leapfrog, or hop, skip, and jump, through the Holy Scriptures, which were written book by book?

When the local clergyman masters the Bible as it was written, a book at a time, the chief benefits accrue to the people. From such a fertile field as the two parts of Samuel the interpreter can draw materials for all kinds of helpful and uplifting sermons. Some of the countless possibilities appear in the Table of Contents of the present volume. First and Second Samuel deal with a wide range of human interests, unfolding on a smaller scale and with slower tempo a series of dramatic episodes that concern almost every important problem now before us in the United States. All the while the narrative centers round two main factors: human need and divine power. These two form the axis round which all true preaching still revolves.

Throughout the two parts of Samuel the undergirding idea

[7] II Kings 6:17.

appears to be this: In days of rebuilding, the leader of the nation needs to discover and to carry out the will of God. This practical philosophy still holds true. "In His will is our peace." In proclaiming this high truth week after week, let us do so concretely, not abstractly. In the books of Samuel we can see how the Lord promotes His cause through persons much like ourselves. If we approach the sacred record with open eyes we shall discover that even the noblest of our heroes proves to be, in Wordsworth's phrase,

> A creature not too bright or good
> For human nature's daily food.

This kind of pulpit work calls for what Horace Bushnell terms "the individualizing power." To many of us Bushnell stands out as the strongest of all American preachers. His practical philosophy about our lifework emerges in three papers that every student of the preacher's craft should know almost by heart. One of these essays Bushnell entitles "Our Gospel a Gift to the Imagination"; another, "The Training of the Pulpit Manward"; a third, "Pulpit Talent." This last article includes the following words of wisdom:

Now and then a man has capital enough for wholesale preaching, but the particular manner of a retail delivery, both in preaching and in trade, is far more apt to succeed, and the success to be more real and reliable. Hence also it is that a great many young men die out in their generalities and huge overgrown subjects, and a great many others, who appear to be meager and want caliber, going to work in this hopeful way of economy, will even preach better possibly, and more effectively, than if they were more profusely endowed. They will at least be saved from the folly of trying to do something so great in the general as to do nothing at all in particular.[8]

[8] *Building Eras* (Scribner, 1910), pp. 197-98.

Part One

THE PASTOR WHO GUIDES IN REBUILDING

FIRST SAMUEL, CHAPTERS 1-12

CHAPTER 1

THE RELIGION OF A BABY'S HOME

I Samuel 1:1–2:11

THIS BIBLICAL NARRATIVE ABOUT WAR AND REBUILDING STARTS WITH the home of a baby boy. So does the Book of Exodus. That earlier part of the Bible shows the beginnings of the Hebrew nation. Undergirding each of these books rests the idea of God. His way of building up a nation, or of rebuilding, calls for a mighty leader, a man of faith. In the development of such a leader, God begins with the family, for the home of God's future leader is the most important spot on earth.

In many quarters of State and Church there seems to be a dearth of strong leaders. The reason may be that we have neglected Christian nurture in the home. If we wish to have streams ever flowing through the valleys, so as to insure bountiful harvests of fruit and grain, we must watch over the springs high on the hills and mountains. Hence there is a call for a revival of concern about religion in the home. The first chapter of Samuel provides one of the best starting points we could find.

1. *The future leader is born into a religious home* (vv. 1-8). Instead of dealing with the family abstractly, or else discussing thousands of households all at once, the Bible fixes our attention on a single home. There the father and mother look on religion as the chief concern of mortals here below. In terms of today we would say they stand out as loyal members and supporters of the local church. Hence we may think of this household as typical of many others. Especially should we remember that this record appears in the Scriptures because from this home the Lord God planned to bring His chosen leader, Samuel.

19

In the religion of this family the husband stands out as the head. He shows his loyalty to God by loving Hannah, his wife. He attends divine services at the appointed time. He contributes liberally to the support of the church. He likewise encourages the other members of the household to attend and contribute. Such is the beginning of what we know about the home background of God's chosen leader. In certain respects the picture reminds us of the Scottish families that nourished such future missionaries as David Livingstone and John G. Paton.

That Hebrew home, however, proved to be far from perfect. Even the best of households must "have this treasure in earthen vessels." The choicest treasure within any family must be the religion that comes down from above. The place where religion makes its earthly abode may be far from ideal. As with the household of many an African chief, the home where little Samuel was to be born suffered from polygamy. Perhaps for this reason, the husband did not fully understand the wife whom he loved most of all. Listen to his words of protest when Hannah wept because she had no child: "Why is thy heart grieved? am not I better to thee than ten sons?" No! A thousand times, No! The Lord God has put in the heart of every normal woman a desire to become a mother. The more a wife loves and reveres the head of the family, the more she longs to bear sons who will carry on his name and his work. If through no fault of her own she must go through the years without children, she ought to be sure of her husband's sympathy. Shame on you, sir, for lack of understanding!

With all its religion the childless home may be unhappy. In fact, the gloom may spring from the piety. Even in the earliest times the Hebrews looked on childlessness as a misfortune. They learned that truth from the God who delighted to be known as Father. Hence they encouraged every growing girl to prepare her heart for the day when she would become a wife and a mother. When the passing years brought Hannah a loving husband, but no little child, she must have envied other women who could become mothers. Whatever the reason, she wept. If such a philosophy seems strange today, the reason may be that we think of marriage apart from motherhood, and from God.

In the home, as elsewhere, God has a way of granting His people what they covet. If a husband and wife become so obsessed about money, or pleasure, that they deliberately refuse to let a little one come into their home, the Heavenly Father may grant their desire—and send leanness into their souls. When at last they awake to the emptiness and loneliness of a house without a child, they may discover that the opportunity for earth's highest joy has gone forever.

> Of all sad words or tongue or pen,
> The saddest are these: "It might have been!"

All the while our hearts go out to every woman who must pass through life without clasping to her bosom the child of her dreams.

2. *The future leader is born into the home of a praying woman* (vv. 9-11). When her heart is breaking, how does Hannah find comfort? With all her disappointment and grief she comes to the house of God. There she pours out her soul unto the Lord. What a beautiful description of prayer! Amid the turmoil and chaos of the era that we associate with the Judges, many a good woman must have come to church with all sorts of sorrows. Is it not ever so? At the City Temple in London, Joseph Parker used to declare that every pew contained at least one broken heart. Especially in our days scarred by war and its aftermath, the Lord God keeps saying to His Church: "Comfort ye, comfort ye my people."

The prayer of this disconsolate woman will repay careful study. First she states the facts, which have to do with the desires of her

21

heart. Then she utters a petition. Last of all she makes a vow. Doubtless her petition appears only in outline. Even so, her way of approaching the mercy seat makes us feel that she had learned to pray. Her spirit and her pleas remind us of those glowing words in the New Testament: "Let us therefore draw near with boldness unto the throne of grace, that we may receive mercy, and may find grace to help us in time of need."[1]

Why do we Protestant ministers not teach our people how to pray? Sometimes we scold them for not bringing their burdens and their problems to the God who delights to hear His children's pleas. More often we exhort them to pray without ceasing. Seldom do we show them how. In Chicago the pastor of a large Lutheran congregation reports that 90 per cent of his people have set up family altars. How has he prevailed on almost four thousand members to engage in regular family devotions? He has gone into their homes, one after another, and there has led his friends in setting up a family altar. Would that every woman like Hannah could have such a "ministering shepherd"!

3. *The home of the future leader needs a faithful pastor* (vv. 12-18). To be exact, we should think of Eli as a priest. For practical purposes, however, we can regard him as a "ministering shepherd." In much the same fashion we often refer to the prophets as preachers. The business of the prophet was to represent God before men; the work of the priest was to represent the people before God. In order to stand in their stead at the community altar and offer sacrifices on their behalf, the priest had to know their needs and cares. All of that still holds true of God's undershepherd. For example, many a local pastor excels in "personal counseling." This blessed work is new only in name, for Eli "counseled" with weeping Hannah and later with her growing son.

When the woman with the breaking heart came to the sanctu-

[1] Heb. 4:16.

ary, she found the pastor at home and ready to help. She rightly expected him to show concern for her, a friend in distress. She also looked to him for expert aid in solving her personal problem. In our own day, such brokenhearted women, as well as disconsolate men, abound on every side. Every parish needs an Eli who will stand ready to serve as a friend and personal counselor. Who else can take such loving care of heart-weary folk, with all their memories and their fears? Who but the pastor can appear in their stead before God?

Eli concerned himself with the burdens of a single breaking heart. He knew that his world had lost the way to God and that he ought to lead in the work of national rebuilding. He could see on every side the debris of what had been torn down during the chaotic days of the Judges. But doubtless he had also learned the central importance of the godly home. At any rate, he took time to deal with the sorrows of a childless wife. How else could he have done so much to assure the coming of better days for the fatherland? Our own times call for a renewal of pastoral concern like that of the venerable Hebrew priest.

Unfortunately, that physician of the soul erred in his diagnosis. Twice in this Hebrew book the same "pastor" tried to interpret a person's needs. Each time he failed to read the symptoms correctly. Unlike some of us who report cases from life, he acknowledged both of his errors. Better still, he sought and found corrective guidance from above. Then he could approach each problem with an assurance born of faith. Why should any of us "ministering shepherds" pose as infallible? Can we not learn from Eli that such a woman as Hannah longs for human sympathy and for access to God. If Eli had prayed before he tried to diagnose her case, he might not have erred.

Eli thought that the woman was intoxicated. Soon he discovered that she was simply pouring out her heart to the Lord. Likewise, at Pentecost the bystanders declared that the apostles were drunk, whereas they were filled with the Holy Spirit. When Paul stood before Agrippa, canny Festus exclaimed, "Thou art mad; thy much learning is turning thee mad." As a matter of fact, the apostle was filled with zeal from above. Who among us has not been guilty of such mistaken judgments? One Person, and only one, has never made any pastoral mistakes. In the days of His flesh our Lord "knew what was in man." So He does now. Through the Holy Spirit, He stands ready to guide every personal counselor.

Despite the unfortunate beginning, the woman's conference with the "ministering shepherd" led to a note of triumph. After she had convinced him that she had come in quest of God, she found in Eli a true friend and helper. Better still, she discovered that God had heard her prayer and that He would grant her desire. Before she went back to her home, she received the benediction of God's peace. Should not every woman with a bruised spirit, as well as every man, find at the local church a kind and skillful physician of the soul? Should not every expectant mother dedicate her unborn babe to the service of God? If we had in each community the right sort of pastor, we might have in Church and State the right sort of leaders.

4. *The godly home welcomes the birth of the future leader* (vv. 19-20). In the heart of Mother Hannah joy abounds, not because her wee son is destined to become famous, but because he has been born well and strong. In the right sort of family circle what other event can compare with the advent of the first-born son? Is he not the answer to prayer, and the child of faith? Was not baby Samuel conceived and nurtured in the spirit of love and hope? From the very day of his birth did he not serve as the visible token of God's invisible grace? Where some other desolate waif seems to be "damned into the world," because of the godless passions that attend his conception and birth, wee baby Samuel was blessed of God before he was born.

5. *The little one is publicly dedicated to God* (vv. 21-28). To dedicate a child means that the human custodians place their choicest treasure in the hands from which it has come. They ask the Heavenly Father to use the babe for the advancement of His Kingdom and to guide them in carrying out His will for the home. To consecrate a child signifies that God "makes holy" what His people have set apart for His use. Many a so-called "consecration service" really consists of dedication. Whatever the descriptive title, the value of such a ceremony depends largely on the faith of those who bring the child to God for His blessing.

The baby Samuel[2] was dedicated to God before he was conceived in the womb. No doubt he was committed to the Lord every night as he lay snuggling unseen by human eye. Surely he was given to God on the day of his birth. After all those personal and family vows, he appears to have been publicly dedicated to the Lord when he was weaned. In the Holy Land the weaning of a child was often postponed. Because of the climate, and the difficulty of rearing a little child, the weaning might not take place until the baby was three years old.[3] By that time, says Horace Bushnell, more has been done to affect the little one's character and destiny than will be wrought in all the years that follow.[4]

According to present-day research, a Hebrew child was considered "exempt from religious duties during the first three years of his life. . . . During those three years, a child was thought of as a newly planted tree whose fruit was not to be eaten until the fourth had come around. . . . This [idea] was based on a rabbinical exegesis of Leviticus 19:23, 24."[5]

[2] For the meaning of Samuel, "The Name of God," see Samuel R. Driver, *Notes on the Hebrew Text of the Books of Samuel* (Oxford, 1890), pp. 13-15.

[3] For such a case see II Macc. 7:27.

[4] See *Christian Nurture* (London, 1872), pp. 153, 161.

[5] Lewis J. Sherrill, *The Rise of Christian Education* (Macmillan, 1944), pp. 48, 313.

The public dedication of little Samuel drew from the lips of Hannah some of the most beautiful words ever uttered by a joyous mother. In the last two verses of our chapter she voices her exultation because of answered prayer. At this stage the biblical account reaches its climax. The dominant verbs repay careful study. Especially in the Hebrew, they show how the mother rejoices in her child as the gift of God and how she gives him back into the hands of her Lord. In the original tongue these verbs carry all sorts of overtones. Even in the English they provide a starting point for an uplifting message for Mother's Day or any other special time when one wishes to uphold the biblical ideals about the home.

The closing verses appear prominently in two autobiographies that every minister can read with enjoyment and profit. Although the authors must have differed in many ways, their books are alike in voicing concern for the everyday work of the pastor. The first of these autobiographies is by Theodore L. Cuyler.[6] In Brooklyn he attained distinction as a beloved pastor. At the end of thirty happy years in the Lafayette Avenue Presbyterian Church he presented to the congregation a memorial window honoring his mother. On the window he instructed the artist to depict Hannah with her child, and he chose the inscription: "As long as he liveth I have lent him to the Lord."

These glowing words stand out still more boldly in one of our most interesting current books, the autobiography of Bishop Edwin Holt Hughes.[7] When his eldest son and namesake was being set apart as a deacon, the father represented the family. Afterward, when the son was being ordained as a Methodist clergyman, his mother delivered the charge. In words of tenderness and charm she told about the "Mother's Bible within our larger Bible." She said that with the coming of their first-born

---

[6] *Recollections of a Long Life*, American Tract Society, 1902.

[7] *I Was Made a Minister*, Abingdon-Cokesbury, 1943.

son both she and the bishop had dedicated the infant to the service of God. All the while she must have been thinking in terms of Hannah. Here follows a portion of the charge by Mother Hughes:

In essence, this story is our own. . . . We gave you to God. We have never taken our gift away from him. . . . We have not felt that in giving you to God we have taken you away from ourselves. Rather have we felt that since the day when you concluded to preach the gospel of his grace and love, you have been ours more than ever—because our parenthood is itself from God, with whom we reverently and gladly share his own gift. . . .

It does not seem long since that morning when God placed you in my arms. I had no feeling then that you left his arms when you came to mine. Again tonight, as I have so often done, I place you in the arms of God. I have no feeling now that you leave my arms when I place you in his. You are my son the more because you are his son the more. I gladly give you to Christ—utterly and forever. You are to be the Saviour's minister. He will keep you, guide you, comfort you, strengthen you. If by his providence I go to the Heavenly Home before you do, I shall wait for your coming in the proud confidence that, even as once you came back to me with the decoration of honor on the worn coat of a young soldier, so then you will come to me with the badge of the Lord Jesus upon your heart, and may its inscription be, "Well done, good and faithful servant!" [8]

6. *The godly home makes the growing child happy* (2:1-11). In order to complete our picture of this happy biblical household, let us glance at the opening paragraph of the second chapter. Here we must proceed somewhat by inference, as we shall not find the poem easy to interpret. However, we learn from it more than a little about the joys of a home that welcomes a little baby boy. The song ascribed to Hannah sounds like the Magnificat of

[8] *Ibid.,* pp. 256-58.

the Virgin Mother.[9] Hannah may have learned that hymn of praise from her mother. Surely she did not compose the song herself, just as Mary did not indite the Magnificat. Whatever the source of Hannah's paean, her beautiful words voice the spirit that fills the heart of a happy mother while she sings at the cradle of her first-born son.

To us matter-of-fact Americans the hymn may seem strange. It rejoices wholly in God, and says nothing about the mother or her babe. However, such an objective song of thanksgiving accords with the spirit of the Old Testament. Almost everywhere the Hebrew Bible teaches the children of men to think mainly about God. In the song of Hannah the first three verses tell of His glory, the next five rejoice in His power, and the last three exult in His approaching triumph. Thus the happy mother seems to have sung more wisely than she knew. Through her son as leader of the nation, God was making ready to deliver His people. What a beautiful atmosphere of joy in which to rear a little lad!

In the religious training of the child do we attach sufficient importance to the climate that prevails in the home? At the fireside should not the future leader start thinking about God and life in terms of peace and joy, as well as hope? In these later days why do we seldom hear a mother singing praises to God while she works with her hands? Would not such happy memories linger with her children long after she falls asleep? Would not the blessings of the Triune God likewise descend on the husband and father? Some such philosophy of domestic bliss once induced our leading soprano to say concerning her pastor: "He must have a happy life at home. He often refers to the family circle and to little children. Whenever he does so, he looks radiant." Why not? Should he not find heaven near in the home where his wife sings her child to sleep?

[9] Luke 1:46-55.

Pause now to glance back over these opening paragraphs of First Samuel. Notice the succession of pictures, one to a paragraph. Look in turn at (1) the religion in the home, with the father as the head; (2) the wife with her broken heart, as she longs for the coming of a child; (3) the pastor with his love for God and his concern for a woman beside herself with grief; (4) the child born into a loving home sanctified by his mother's prayer; (5) the church publicly welcoming the little child in the name of God; and (6) the mother singing praises to the Giver of every good and perfect gift.

What an ascending series! Through the home and the church our God prepares the leader who is to guide in rebuilding the nation. Is not such preparation of its youth the need of many a home, and many a land, today?

CHAPTER 2

THE EXCESSES OF YOUNG CLERGYMEN

I Samuel 2:12-36

THE REMAINDER OF THE SECOND CHAPTER IN FIRST SAMUEL MAKES sorry reading. Indeed, we sometimes ask why these records appear in the Scriptures. One reason may be to set up danger signals for church leaders, since the very same pitfalls continue to lurk in the pathway of every young minister. "Wherefore let him that thinketh he standeth take heed lest he fall." [1] Another reason may be to show by contrast the nobility of young Samuel. In this passage the writer points to Samuel five different times,[2] in each case setting him over against the young scions of Eli.

Thus we have a study in black and white, or rather, in white and black. In the first and third chapters the author shows the good character whom we are to remember most clearly. In between these two bright scenes comes the dark account of young men whom we are not to admire. In much the same fashion the writer of the First Psalm points out the fruitful tree and then the worthless chaff. So does our Lord show us the house on the rock before we see the house on the sand. According to a current master of psychology,[3] a speaker ought to place in the forefront what he wishes the hearer to recall most vividly. Here in First Samuel the dominant purpose is positive. Hence the word pictures of a happy home and a growing boy seem all the brighter be-

---

[1] I Cor. 10:12.
[2] I Sam. 2:11, 18, 21*b*, 26; 3:1*a*.
[3] See Harry L. Hollingworth, *The Psychology of the Audience* (American Book, 1935), pp. 98, 100.

cause of the intervening shadows. Now let us look at the shadows.

1. *The wrong attitude toward God* (vv. 12-17). "The sons of Eli were base men; they knew not the Lord." What an indictment of young men set apart for leadership in public worship! The basic fact about any man is the character of his God and his attitude toward that Deity. This is doubly true of a religious leader. According to Woodrow Wilson, himself a son of the manse, the minister's work consists mainly in "being," not in doing or speaking. In the life of a clergyman "being" springs from religion within the heart. If a pastor does not know God personally and well, his life may be base. What then are the besetting sins of young clergymen? According to our passage, they are three. Let us put the chief one first.

The root of all ministerial evils appears to be unbelief. Those two young priests must have had no religious experience of their own. If they knew the Lord at all, it was only at second hand, and from afar. They tried to keep their religion in their father's name, being good by proxy. With the patriarch Job either of them might have exclaimed:

I had heard of thee by the hearing of the ear.

But neither of Eli's sons could have completed the saying:

Now mine eye seeth thee:
Wherefore I abhor myself,
And repent in dust and ashes.[4]

Those two young fellows were the sons of a man who knew the living God, but still they looked on work for Him as only a job for pay. This is what we mean today by professionalism.

Coupled with their unbelief went greed. In any man the love of money for its own sake may prove to be a millstone round

[4] Job 42:5-6.

31

his neck. Above all, in the life of a minister the lure of gold may lead to disaster. In order to be used by the Lord a clergyman needs to look on his sacred office as a heaven-sent opportunity for service, even for sacrifice. But those young fellows seem to have gone into their lifework for what they could get out of it in the way of gain. Whenever the ministry of God becomes only a job for hire, the Church goes from bad to worse. Then there must be a reformation.

A kindred evil we term "irreverence." "The men despised the offering of the Lord." The word translated "despise" does not mean to hate but to treat with indifference. When a worldly minded fellow handles the vessels of the sanctuary day after day, he becomes a sort of foreman. He acts as though the Church of God consisted solely of machinery. He begins to look on his work as a racket or a farce. "Familiarity breeds contempt." Whatever the reason, some of us ministers have gained the reputation of being irreverent. By way of contrast let us turn again to young Samuel.

2. *The right attitude toward God* (vv. 18-21). "But Samuel ministered before the Lord." Despite the vile example of the two young fellows set apart to represent the holiness of God, the boy Samuel kept his hands clean and his heart pure. In fact, he must have begun to do all that before he knew the Lord as his God. If so, action led to deepening experience. This is said to be the working theory of the Jews, and of the Roman Catholics. As Dean Lewis J. Sherrill makes clear, "the Torah can be learned by being obeyed." [5] For a few years the religion of the little Samuel may have been secondhand. In like manner a little fellow today learns to sing:

> Jesus loves me! this I know,
> For the Bible tells me so.

[5] *The Rise of Christian Education* (Macmillan, 1944), p. 51; note also the references.

All the while the lad ought to be growing religiously, as well as otherwise. The words about Samuel make us think of the saying about the boy Jesus. Each of them "grew before the Lord." The Boy of Nazareth "increased . . . in favor with God and man."[6] A good child can grow up with evil men, much as a white lily may emerge from the blackest muck. More than a little depends on the character of the original stock. Even when forced to dwell among older fellows as base as the sons of Eli, a lad like Samuel keeps on serving the God of his mother and father. In army and navy training camps, here at home and on countless battlefields beyond the seven seas, young men who had loved God back at home kept on being loyal despite all the seductions of a world at war.

3. *The wrong attitude toward other people* (vv. 22-26). The conduct of those two young priests became so rank that their indulgent old father felt obliged to protest: "Ye make the Lord's people to transgress." Those "religious" young leaders sadly abused their privileges. Their particular sin appears to have been impurity. Thus the chapter brings out three evils that beset worldly minded clergymen: abuse of power, love of money, and lust after women. According to an army officer of high rank, these were the most frequent causes during the second World War for the dishonorable discharge of young chaplains.

The comparative rarity of gross ministerial offenses makes them stand out all the more glaringly. Obviously, no man in our profession can claim to be flawless. Nevertheless, perhaps only one in five hundred stoops to deeds of infamy like those of Eli's sons. Mayhap only one in a thousand brings public disgrace on the name of Christ and His Church. At the same time, some of us may try to live in a sort of No Man's Land. We neither take our stand with young Samuel, who was out and out for God, nor

[6] Luke 2:52 (A.V.); see also Luke 2:40. Cf. I Sam. 2:21*b*, 26.

do we stoop to the baseness of Eli's sons, who became the bond-servants of Satan. "Choose you this day whom ye will serve."

Note that the writer puts first the sins against God, and then the wrongs against people. Thus he states the cause before the effect. As a rule the Scriptures put the first thing first. In the Ten Commandments, for instance, why does the Table about duties to God precede the section about duties to men? Because the First Table provides the foundation for the Second. In like manner our Lord speaks of a man's religion in terms of love for his God, and then of love for his neighbor.[7] In giving the priority to the major, not the minor, the Scriptures anticipate the findings of modern scholars. Savants who specialize in the psychology of attention have learned the practical wisdom of presenting the large idea first, and then repeating it at intervals.[8] Strange to tell, this method proves climactic. The reason may be that we mortals show more concern for the human than for the divine. Hence our interest grows as we proceed. For an example, look at the present chapter.

4. *The wrong attitude toward unworthy leaders* (vv. 27-36). An unknown seer pronounced the judgment of God on the father of those faithless young priests. Eli should have curbed their excesses. In sooth, he should never have permitted those sons to don the priestly robes. Even after he had inducted them into office, he should have unfrocked them as soon as he found them incorrigible. He must have known that the welfare of the Church transcends everything personal. But like many another doting father, Eli seems to have had more influence over everyone else than over his sons.

These facts afford a warning for the Church today. On every hand there appears to be a dearth of candidates for the ministry. Hence we may be tempted occasionally to ordain a moral misfit.

[7] Exod. 20:2-17; Matt. 22:37-40.

[8] See Albert T. Poffenberger, *Psychology in Advertising*, McGraw-Hill, 1932.

When once we have laid hands upon the wrong sort of fellow, we seem loath to take away his commission. If we erred in only a single case out of five hundred, or even a thousand, that would be one too many. How can we expect to enjoy the favor of God, or even the respect of men, if we retain as a spiritual leader a fellow as base as one of Eli's sons? If such an indictment sounds harsh, search the records of the Church!

Over against those two unworthy priests behold a figure far more vast than any other person who appears in the books of Samuel. Indeed, certain scholars assure us that the mighty Person who emerges near the end of our chapter must be the coming Messiah.[9] Note the majesty of these words, which come from God: "I will raise me up a faithful priest, . . . and I will build him a sure house." Whatever the original reference, these glowing promises have found their supreme fulfillment in that "merciful and faithful high priest" who stands out triumphantly in the Epistle to the Hebrews.[10] Wherever He has His way in the Church that He died to redeem, there can be no place for such leaders as the sons of Eli.

At certain stages in the history of the Christian Church this matter of clerical immorality has loomed large. In Europe before the Reformation think of Tetzel and other "churchmen" with their ecclesiastical greed; of Alexander VI and other popes with their ecclesiastical licentiousness; of St. Peter's in Rome and St. Mark's in Venice, with their mechanistic professionalism. Many of us rightly deplore the irreverence that today prevails in certain Protestant sanctuaries, but some of us have never witnessed elsewhere so much ecclesiastical callousness as at St. Peter's in Rome, the fountainhead of Roman Catholicism. And yet our recent books about public worship laud the Romanists,

[9] See Charles A. Briggs, *Messianic Prophecy* (Scribner, 1891), pp. 122, 490; and Willis J. Beecher, *The Prophets and the Promise* (Crowell, 1905), pp. 300-1.
[10] See Heb. 2:17, 4:14, 5:1-3, *et al.*

as though they had achieved a monopoly on holiness in approaching God.

Think, too, about modern history. In France before the Revolution of 1789, and in Russia prior to the cataclysm of 1917, the low estate of the clergy seems to have been largely responsible for the temporary overthrow of the Church. Much the same kind of unworthy leadership seems to have prevailed in the Roman Church of Latin America. Partly for this reason, organized religion has become a stench in the nostrils of thoughtful men in that "other America." Notwithstanding all this, let us search our own hearts before we start casting stones. The time has come for another Protestant Reformation.

What then do we demand of every young clergyman? We expect him to have a religion of his own and to keep himself unspotted from the world. Among the clergy, even more than with laymen, religion consists in right relations with God and leads to right relations with men. Religion also brings a man into right relations with himself. To us as Christians religion means being right through our Lord Jesus as Saviour and King. In terms of the chapter now at hand, religion means being like Samuel, not like the sons of Eli. They were "base men; they knew not the Lord."

The excesses of unworthy church leaders often resemble the debaucheries of other worldlings. Nevertheless, when a leader in the Church departs from the ways of God the effect on public morals proves far more serious than when other men transgress. What a travesty of religion when the man who ought to set an example of holy living becomes a purveyor of vice! Thus he shows his fellows the enormity of sin. This familiar word "sin" points to a man's way of putting himself out of right relations with God, with others, and with himself. All the while the main problem lies deeper: how can the wrongdoer get right with God, with others, and with himself? To this question we shall return as we proceed through the books of Samuel.

For a study in ministerial immorality turn to Nathaniel Hawthorne's masterpiece, *The Scarlet Letter,* which seems to be the best piece of prose writing on our side of the water thus far. Religiously, this novel should lead every clergyman to search his conscience. After all, what does our war-blasted world need most from the Church? A generation of ministerial leaders as pure and high-minded as Samuel! Even the Almighty could not rebuild the nations if He had to depend on "foremen" like the sons of Eli. Fortunately, He stands ready to transform the weakest and the worst of His ministering servants. "If any man is in Christ, he is a new creature: the old things are passed away; behold, they are become new." [11]

[11] II Cor. 5:17.

CHAPTER 3

THE RELIGION OF A GROWING BOY

1 Samuel 3

ONCE AGAIN THE NARRATIVE MAKES US THINK OF THE THIRD GOSPEL. The lad's experience in the sanctuary resembles that of the boy Jesus in a much larger temple.[1] Instead of dwelling on the likenesses and differences in the two experiences, however, let us confine our attention to the religion of the growing Hebrew boy. We do not know his age, but we may think of him as about twelve or thirteen years old.[2] That seems to be the best time for a growing lad to enlist in the ranks of God's visible Church. From this viewpoint let us note the stages in Samuel's experience.

1. *How the growing boy discovers God* (vv. 1-9). To be accurate, let us say that God revealed Himself to Samuel, and that the boy responded gladly. Thus the experience led to what we know as "child conversion." Here again we long for words more exact. "Child conversion" suggests that the lad had fallen into iniquity and that he had repented. As a matter of fact, he appears to have passed through an open gateway along the path that he had been treading ever since he learned to toddle. Why does not some student of the Bible suggest a name for such a religious experience? Thus far the best title seems to be Confirmation.

The facts about Samuel remind us that in the worst of times a boy may be good in the sight of God. For example, think of

[1] Luke 2:41-52.
[2] See Alfred Edersheim, *The Life and Times of Jesus the Messiah* (Longmans, Green, n.d.), I, 235.

Joseph over against his older brothers, and of Ruth among the coarse men of Moab. In the time of young Samuel what we know as the Holy Land had become chaotic. "The word of the Lord was rare in those days; there was no frequent vision." In that era of the Judges the vast majority of the people had been striving to get along without God. Doubtless they supposed that they had succeeded. Here and there, however, as in the "little town of Bethlehem," loyal souls held to the faith of their fathers. Those stalwart believers included the father and mother of Samuel. Is not this God's normal way of preparing seed corn for the extension of His Kingdom?

The passage likewise brings out the Hebrew ideal of boyhood. Much the same conception has since obtained among pious folk in Scotland and Holland. There the stress falls on such old-fashioned virtues as obedience and industry, thrift and liberality, promptness and courtesy. For a living example of these qualities, turn to young Samuel. When suddenly awakened out of a sound sleep, he immediately responded to the call. He did so the second time, and even the third, with never a sign of petulance. What an exacting test! "The child who learns to do small things well when he is small gets the best training for doing big things well when he is big."

Nevertheless, the account brings to light one serious lack: "Samuel did not yet know the Lord." Whatever else these words may tell, they suggest that we church folk must have been receiving into our membership more than a few boys and girls, as well as men and women, without a heart-knowledge of God. If so, their religion must be secondhand. In time they will fall away from the church, and we shall wonder why. This holds true not only of evil folk, such as the sons of Eli, but also of "good, moral men," who may rely on the testimony of others as a substitute for firsthand experience of the living God. This kind of church member appears in our Lord's parable: "He has no root in himself, he does not last." [3]

Whatever the facts about any particular case, every lad or lass of ten or twelve years needs to know the Lord directly. That may have been why the Hebrew poet sang,

> Oh satisfy us in the morning with thy lovingkindness,
> That we may rejoice and be glad all our days,

and why the sage exhorted, "Remember now thy Creator in the days of thy youth." [4] At the age of seventeen a lad may go out from home to swim in deep waters. Then he will need more than the assurance that his parents know how to swim. Once the headmaster of a famous boys' school complained to Dean L. B. R. Briggs, of Harvard: "In three months your University undoes all that we have accomplished in four long years." With his disarming smile the Dean made answer: "In four years you should build up strength enough to last here more than three months."

Every schoolman knows that many a teen-age boy lacks a religion of his own. The dear lad may strive to live on borrowed faith, but soon he will run out of such funds. Before he goes away from home, why can he not say to his mother or father: "Now I believe, not because of thy teaching, for I know God myself"? [5] In the church school every growing boy needs as mentor an older man who knows how to introduce his young friend to Jesus Christ. Fortunate is the Bible school where every class of boys older than six or eight years has a male teacher who loves to serve as an undershepherd. Blessed is the congregation where the ordained minister never becomes so busy as to neglect any growing boy. After two happy years in the work of the parish

[3] Matt. 13:21*a* (Moffatt).
[4] Psa. 90:14; Eccl. 12:1*a* (A.V.).
[5] John 4:42 (paraphrased).

40

a young clergyman reports that his most gratifying experiences have come in dealing with boys the age of young Samuel. His wife has found equal joy in being a big sister to the growing girls.

All the while God stands ready to make Himself known. The initiative must rest with Him: "The Lord called Samuel." Then God waited for the lad's response. This procedure seems to have mystified Eli. He may have thought the boy had been dreaming. Perhaps that was the case, for we do not know how the Lord called Samuel. Somehow or other, despite the misapprehensions of us older folk, God has a way of revealing Himself to a growing lad. The Lord can likewise open the eyes of the older "counselor," so that he recognizes his error in judgment. As he did when dealing with Hannah, Eli acknowledged his mistake. Then he was able rightly to interpret the will of God. In our own time, also, the personal counselor needs to beware lest he overestimate the spiritual attainments of a growing boy, and likewise underestimate his spiritual possibilities.[6]

2. *How God tests the reality of a boy's religion* (vv. 10-14). Samuel's discovery of God led to an unwelcome task. To his dismay the lad found that he must become the messenger of God's judgment. He learned that oncoming doom would fall on his friend and benefactor, aged Eli, as well as on the land that both of them loved. Through years to come the people would have to suffer because of Eli's failure to curb his wicked sons.

For a parallel case turn to Isaiah, who seems to have been a few years older than Samuel at the time of his soul's awakening.[7] With Isaiah, as with the younger lad, the revelation of God's blessing led to a commission full of judgment. Throughout all the years to come, the experience at his call would linger in each man's heart as proof that he and his work belonged to God.

What a searching test of a lad's integrity! Sometime between

---

[6] For modern examples of "child conversion" see Blackwood, *Evangelism in the Home Church* (Abingdon-Cokesbury, 1942), pp. 36-39.

[7] See Isa. 6:1-13, especially vv. 9-13.

the coming of night and the dawning of day the boy Samuel meets with God and hears the call to become a messenger of judgment. When the morning breaks, what will he do? Will he tell Eli about the uplifting call or about the oncoming doom? Will the lad speak the truth, or evade the issue? Does he know that a man sins as grievously if he keeps silent when he ought to speak as if he speaks when he ought to keep silent? Whatever the rationale, young Samuel passed with distinction the first test of his new religious experience. Then he continued to speak the truth, whatever the cost. How otherwise could he have served through the years as one of God's noblest prophets?

3. *How God enables His young servant to perform an unwelcome duty* (vv. 15-18). "Samuel lay until the morning, and opened the doors of the house of the Lord." As in the career of many a good man since, the fleeting vision of the Lord gave way to a prosaic task. The lad who rejoiced in the sovereignty of God likewise responded to the quiet call of duty. But he did not look upon himself as a hero or a martyr. Whether the call of duty led him to something humble, or something hard, still he did not flinch. In later years, throughout a career full of arduous duties, Samuel never faced a more unwelcome task than that of telling aged Eli about his approaching doom. But first the lad opened the doors of the temple. Thus does life bring an occasional crisis amid endless details.

The experiences of a growing boy seldom prove so pleasant as we older folk suppose. Why do we not take our ideas about such things from the Scriptures, including the Old Testament? Those ancient narratives hold the mirror up to our human nature as it appears in the eyes of God. They do not show existence on earth as one endless succession of "sweetness and light." Why then do we sometimes try to take an elective course in our religion? Why do we strive to dodge everything dark and gloomy?

A warning of this kind has come from a friendly observer of religion in the States. For a number of years Professor A. A. Bowman, of Glasgow, taught philosophy at Princeton University. When about to leave the States he told a group of friends that he had formed two unfavorable impressions about religion on our side of the water. He said that many of us neglected the Old Testament, and that we made religion seem too easy. This judgment from the leading Scottish philosopher of his day should bid us pause and search our hearts. Do we need to learn from young Samuel the ruggedness of true religion? "Suffer hardship with me, as a good soldier of Jesus Christ." [8]

4. *How God blesses the ministry of one whom He has called* (3:19–4:1a). This brief section looks out over the years to come, especially those of the prophet. In doing so, the account begins with the boy at his "conversion." Like the holy child Jesus, the Hebrew lad kept on growing in wisdom and stature, and in favor with God and man. When the record states that God was "with" the lad, the expression makes us think of young Joseph. He too rejoiced in the nearness of God, in His guidance, and in His blessing. Since young Samuel was destined to become the interpreter of God's will for the nation and the Church, the stress here falls on the reality of his spoken words: The Lord "did let none of his words fall to the ground."

In the course of time all Israel "knew that Samuel was established to be a prophet of the Lord." In the Hebrew this word "established" comes from the same root as "Amen." Hence we infer that whenever this man spoke on behalf of God the people knew that the message had come from above. By a sort of sympathetic vibration the hearts of God's children always respond to an authentic word from the throne. In college days some of us used to hear every morning the call of the bell up in the tower. From across the way we could catch the fainter tones of the

[8] II Tim. 2:3.

bell in a church steeple. We knew that the second bell was being rung by no human hands, but that it responded to the message from across the way. The two bells had been attuned alike. So may it be whenever a man of God speaks to his waiting people! "Amen!"

In our days of national and world rebuilding, wherein lies the secret of an effective ministry? We have learned from these early years of Samuel's life that this work demands character, a call, and a commission. As a rule the call of God comes to a youth before he has crossed the threshold of manhood. Whatever the time and the details, the need just now is for the man whom the Lord has chosen and commissioned. Whenever the interpreter speaks in His name, all Israel should know that he has been established as a prophet of the Most High God. Then none of the minister's words will fall to the ground. "Amen!"

Chapter 4

THE PERILS OF PRESENT-DAY WORSHIP

1 Samuel 4

THIS CHAPTER RAISES A NUMBER OF DIFFICULT QUESTIONS. HOWEVER, it contains one clear teaching which dominates the passage. The central truth concerns the abuse of religious symbols. Almost every branch of the Protestant Church of late has shown increasing concern about religious symbols.[1] This movement affords all sorts of possibilities for good. Still it may lead to peril. If there were time we could consider numerous object lessons from the history of the Roman Church. Unfortunately, we have more than enough sorry examples in current Protestantism.

What do we understand by a religious symbol? The term points to a visible sign of God's invisible presence and His redeeming grace. Tokens of God's presence and blessing abounded in the worship of Old Testament times. In dealing with childish folk the Lord made Himself known through symbols. The most beloved of those in the Bible appear in the New Testament. There we find baptism and the Lord's Supper, through which our God appeals to what Bunyan calls the "eye-gate."

At present we are concerned with the symbolism of the Ark. In the twenty-two verses of our present chapter the word "ark" appears twelve times. In each case the term refers to a chest of acacia wood covered with gold. Over the chest hovered two symbolic figures, known as the Cherubim. The Ark was supposed to contain a copy of the Ten Commandments, a pot of manna,

[1] See Thomas A. Stafford, *Christian Symbolism in the Evangelical Churches,* Abingdon-Cokesbury, 1942.

45

and a rod that budded. Those sacred objects pointed back to the presence of God and to the deliverance from Egyptian bondage. Covering the Ark, and illuminated by a mysterious light known as the Shekinah, rested the mercy seat. That signified the grace of God in redeeming men from sin.

Thus far we have been thinking about Hebrew ideals of public worship. Both in the Wilderness and in the Promised Land religion and life were supposed to center round the Ark of the Covenant. In the temporary tabernacle and in the later temple, at the heart of all Hebrew worship the Ark stood supreme. So in a Gothic cathedral everything centers round the altar. According to recent books about public worship[2] many of our Protestant problems will be solved when each local church gives up the Central Bible of Reformation days and substitutes the Central Altar of the Mother Church.

Obviously, people can worship God acceptably through symbols, and they can lose sight of Him through their zeal for forms. Since our purpose now is practical, not controversial, let us take for granted the perils of so-called bibliolatry, as well as those of the no less real "altarolatry." This hybrid term suggests the absurdity of setting up ceremonies as ends in themselves rather than as means of grace. Let us assume that the Ark symbolized the blessings that we enjoy in public worship today. By resorting to metonomy we can think of the Ark as the old-time equivalent of the local church. What then does this fourth chapter of First Samuel teach us about the perils of present-day worship?

1. *In the day of disaster the people of God may put their trust in a religious symbol* (vv. 1b-4). The events now in view took place at Ebenezer, a site whose name meant "Stone of Help." There the people of God suffered a crushing defeat, which must have been as unexpected as our own disaster at Bull Run or at Pearl Harbor. The unlooked-for reverse led the Israelites to

[2] For example, see Scott F. Brenner, *The Way of Worship*, Macmillan, 1944.

think of their religion. Or rather, the disaster made them resort to magic, the use of improper means to attain spiritual ends. As a rule the devices of magic are mechanical rather than vital. The ways of worship become merely a "technique," a pulling of wires. In themselves the means may not be wrong. In fact, the Ark was good. It had come from God. The folly consisted in trusting the thing as a substitute for the Almighty. Thus the means of grace became the ends in worship. "The symbol never saves; only the Presence can save."

In the hour of disaster the thoughts of men turned to the Ark: "Let us fetch the ark of the covenant . . . that it may come among us, and save us." This cry hailed from the "elders," who were the religious leaders of the people. The resort to magic often springs from the lack of worthy leaders. What but magic could you expect from a people whose most active priests were the sons of Eli? In times a little later, when Samuel was present and in control, those very same people never once resorted to the Ark as a substitute for God.

For another example of Hebrew magic turn to the brazen serpent.[3] It had served as a means of blessing in a time of deadly pestilence. As long as that plague raged, if any stricken person looked up to the symbol he lived. Consequently, in the course of later years, people began to worship the brazen serpent. When it became a stumbling block, the brazen serpent had to be destroyed. Centuries afterward, by a sort of literary resurrection, our Lord transformed that oldtime symbol into a means of exalting "the healing Cross."

2. *The people of God lose their religious symbol* (vv. 5-11). Throughout this account of a battle, the so-called children of God appeared in a less pleasing light than the outlandish invaders. When the nominal followers of the Lord beheld the Ark, they shouted. Then the Philistines became so affrighted

---

[3] For a Bible reading use Num. 21:9, II Kings 18:4, John 3:14.

that they exclaimed, "God is come into the camp!" Nevertheless, the invading hosts acquitted themselves like men of might. Ere long they captured the Ark and slew the two unworthy priests. Thus the forces of antigod prevailed over the would-be followers of the Most High.

Apart from the indwelling Presence, of what use was that symbol? First, men said that God was in the Ark. Then they insisted that God *was* the Ark. Later they assumed that the Ark was God. Hence they relied on the Ark as a substitute for the God of their fathers. Is there no such magic in our midst today? For instance, recall some of the prayers that have been coming over the radio. One that issued from a recent incumbent of the White House embodied a plea that we citizens resort to prayer as a panacea. Whenever a zealous leader addresses his public prayer to us as human beings, does he not unwittingly resort to the use of magic? What leader of worship can plead not guilty?

3. *The people of God again meet with disaster* (vv. 12-18); *thus they lose their glory* (vv. 19-22). All of this action reaches its climax in the birth of a baby named Ichabod. The name has won renown through Washington Irving's legend about Ichabod Crane and Whittier's poem about Daniel Webster as Ichabod. To the Hebrews the word meant "No Glory," or more freely, "The Glory Is Departed from Israel." All of this because the Ark of God had been taken. From that hour until the present, whenever God's people have placed their trust in a symbol as a substitute for God, they have run the risk of losing their glory.

The word Ichabod once figured prominently in the religious life of London. At the City Temple, Joseph Parker had become as famous a pulpit orator as our own Henry Ward Beecher. One day in a burst of eloquence Parker declared that if anyone ever preached any other gospel at the City Temple, someone would write across her portals the word of doom, ICHABOD!

One morning in after years the throngs of passers-by were startled to see painted across the front of City Temple that one word ICHABOD!

No one of us would justify or condone such vandalism. We trust that the perpetrator met with British justice swift and stern. Nevertheless, that cowardly deed suggests a serious question: Is it not possible that the most spiritual-minded congregation may lose her glory by forgetting her God? For example, when a downtown church disbands, and the building becomes a dance hall, why not call it "The House of Ichabod"?

The last word, however, does not rest with Ichabod. If we look forward to chapter 7 we shall find the record of a sweeping victory on the field of that former defeat. Thus the site became known as Ebenezer, or "Stone of Help." Where once the Ark of God had been captured, and the cause of the Kingdom had seemed to be lost, within a few years Samuel erected a memorial of victory. He ascribed all the glory to God. Hence we often sing:

> Here I raise mine Ebenezer;
> Hither by Thy help I'm come.

Once in a while every parish minister needs to inquire: How is it with our home church? Does it deserve to be known as Ebenezer, or as Ichabod?

These facts may lead to a sermon. A godly woman at Wilmington, Delaware, loves to recall a message from her pastor some years ago. He took as his text those words about fetching the Ark that it might save. In striking fashion he brought out the folly of relying on any man-made thing as a substitute for the living God. When the children of Israel looked to the Ark for deliverance, they met with defeat and disaster. When they turned back to the Almighty, they went forth to triumph.

Why does the lay hearer recall that sermon after the lapse of years? Because the interpreter led her to see, to feel, and to act.

If he had merely recounted the facts in scholastic jargon, his ponderous "message" would have vanished from her memory before she left the sanctuary. Still we wonder why people do not come to church. They prefer not to be bored!

Give heed to the ablest of our older American writers about homiletics: "Preach little in the general and much in the detail. Preach little on truth and much on truths. Preach rarely on religion but constantly on the facts, the doctrines, the duties, the privileges of religion, . . . till the whole map of Christian faith is outlined and clear. You thus gain the power of pointed preaching." [4]

---

[4] Austin Phelps, *The Theory of Preaching* (Scribner, 1881), p. 289.

CHAPTER 5

THE CHURCH IN A PAGAN COUNTRY

I Samuel 5

THIS CHAPTER BRISTLES WITH DIFFICULTY. AMID ALL ITS PROBLEMS one truth shines out clearly: God requires reverence for the visible symbols of His presence. The record shows how He made this lesson known to people who were engaged in a sort of guerrilla warfare. To us the account may speak concerning the reception of the gospel in lands that we call pagan. At least they have given themselves over to idolatry. In days when we are beginning to think again about taking the Good News to every land for which the Saviour died, it is fitting that we consider this narrative about Dagon. What is likely to occur when the symbols of God's presence confront the chief idol in a non-Christian shrine?

1. *The Church of God comes face to face with idolatry* (vv. 1-5). When the Philistines captured the Ark of the Covenant they took it to Ashdod. That was one of their five main cities, all strung along the Mediterranean Seaboard. Perhaps those victors wished to establish a sort of Pantheon, with a "Congress of Religions." At the local shrine, which they had erected in honor of Dagon, the fish god,[1] they would make room for the Ark, which betokened the presence of the Hebrew Deity. In like manner the devotees of idolatry over in India today would gladly admit our Christ to their temples. They would accord Him due honor as one of their three million gods. To all such proposals

[1] Many scholars think of Dagon as a fish god, others, as an agricultural deity. For our purposes either conjecture will serve.

51

our missionaries have replied, most courteously: "The world has countless religions, but Christianity is not one of them. It must stand alone."

When the Ark was borne into the temple of Dagon, that god made by men fell to the ground. Restored to its pedestal, the idol again went crashing to the floor. This time the handmade god was almost demolished. The resulting scene appears in a picture that the writer once beheld in the Vatican Galleries. At the end of a corridor a large panel represented the interior of an ancient temple. There stood the Ark of God, resplendent in its glory. Before it on the floor, shattered into fragments, lay the remnants of the fish god. What a vivid way of teaching religion to every passer-by!

Without twisting the facts, we can draw a parallel with world-wide missions. From more than one distant land come reports of idols falling down before the Christian gospel. In China and India some of these days the choice will rest between Christ and Communism, not between Him and idolatry. At least among educated folk, contacts with our religion have gone far to do away with the worship of idols. Only here and there, it may be among underprivileged folk, will men and women continue to bow down before handmade gods. Consequently, there comes a question: Are we in the Protestant Church ready and eager to capture all those millions who seem destined to lose faith in their man-made gods? Vile as idolatry may become, with all its loathsome by-products in the way of commercialized vice, the worship of a fish god may prove less pernicious than the belief in no god. When has atheism ever built a shrine, or blessed a seeker?

2. *The presence of the Church may cause the devotees of pagan religions to protest* (vv. 6-12). If the Christian Church were as powerless as some of her critics suppose, no one would object to the advent of Christianity. But if the coming of the Ark causes

Dagon to totter and fall, if the advent of the gospel serves as dynamite to blast the foundations of Asiatic religions, the devotees of idolatry will strive to banish the visible symbols of God's presence. Before the outbreak of World War II the rising tides of nationalism threatened to sweep Christian missions from the Near East and the Far East. Back of the spirit known as nationalism stood the forces of the non-Christian religions. To their dismay the leaders of those other movements found that their false gods could not endure the light that streamed from the face of our Lord.

With still more caution we may draw a parallel with conditions closer home. During the years prior to World War II, Mussolini stole the land of Ethiopia. At once he drove out all the missionaries except the Roman Catholics. When Franco took over the kingship of Spain, he did his utmost to exterminate every vestige of Protestantism. If other and fiercer dictators had been able to carry out their ambitious designs, they might have compelled us Protestants to withdraw our missionary forces from large sections of Asia and Africa, as well as the islands of the sea. In other words, the causes of World War II were closely intertwined with the issue of religious liberty.

Still more recently this whole matter has come to the fore in Latin America.[2] Wherever the Roman Catholic Church constitutes the minority group its leaders welcome religious freedom. For years it has been so here in the States, as well as in Canada. But in large areas of Latin America the hierarchy seems unwilling to tolerate Protestantism as a minority group. In this attitude toward our representatives the Government at Washington appears at times to accept the viewpoint of the Roman Catholics. All the while we wonder why the leaders of the Roman Church in the lands to the south fear the presence of

[2] See George F. Howard, *Religious Liberty in Latin America?* Westminster, 1944.

Evangelical Christianity. Whatever the answer, the people in those lands will not forever accept old-time paganism, even though it has been baptized in the name of the Triune God.

In many a land today the leaders in the government keep asking each other, in effect: "What then shall be done with the Ark of the God of Israel?" In terms of our era, what shall the rulers of the nations do with the Church of Christ? For light on this agelong problem turn to First Samuel. There you will learn anew the wisdom of exalting the Church. Does it not stand as the visible symbol of God's presence in our midst? Where is the land today that does not need the Church of Christ?

CHAPTER 6

THE PROBLEM OF RELIGIOUS LIBERTY

I Samuel 6:1–7:2

AGAIN WE FACE THE QUESTION: WHAT SHALL THE NATION DO WITH
the Church? Historically, we note three different answers. As
Protestants most of us have been taught to believe that both
Church and State belong to God, and that each of them should
recognize the rights of the other. The State should accord the
Church complete liberty in matters of religion. The Church
should train her sons and daughters as loyal citizens of their
country. For a practical example of such dual control over the
same human beings, think of a godly farmer and his wife. He
directs the work out in the fields, and she manages everything
within the house. In all their dealings with children and servants
—if there be any such helpers—the two live and work together
in holy love. As partners they strive to carry out the will of God.

According to a second theory, the Roman Catholic Church
seeks to lord it over the State. That has been the persistent
endeavor of the Roman hierarchy wherever it has held ascend-
ancy. From this point of view study the history of Europe
throughout the Middle Ages. Then by way of contrast think of
the third answer to the question. Over against both the
Protestant Church and the Romanists stands another group.
They insist that the State rule over the Church. At the time of
the Reformation this practical philosophy became known as
Erastianism. Long before the days of Erastus, who was a follower
of Zwingli, the dictators of earth strove to control the souls of
men and women. For a series of object lessons in such tyranny,

study the Book of Exodus, or the first six chapters in Daniel. In later times think of the French Revolution and of the Russian upheaval. Today much the same philosophy of government bids fair to threaten the forces of Protestantism in Turkey and elsewhere abroad. So let us turn to our passage and see how the men there in control dealt with what we call the Church.

1. *The proposal to send the Ark out of the land* (vv. 1-9). What lay back of the suggestion to get rid of the Ark no one now can tell. Practically, every student of world affairs has witnessed something similar. In Turkey and in Iran, in Egypt and in the Far East, secular authorities in the recent past have tried to simplify local situations by curtailing the work of our missionaries. In some places the growing hostility may have been partly due to the mistaken zeal of irresponsible bodies that have antagonized the rulers of those distant lands. As a rule, however, the "rising tide of color" has swept out from deeper sources. Just at present, in the wake of World War II, the matter lies in abeyance. But there can be no reason to believe that the movement loosely known as nationalism has lost its momentum.

2. *The people of Beth-shemesh receive the Ark with gladness* (vv. 10-16). When the people of Beth-shemesh saw the Ark coming into the village their hearts began to sing with joy. Those simple country folk looked upon the Ark as the visible symbol of God's presence, and of His desire to bless. The resulting picture may seem almost idyllic. Stalwart men at their work out in the harvest field. When they behold the Ark they pause to rest and worship. If we could add to the scene the element of love, we should have a complete picture of "what men live by." Work . . . rest . . . love . . . worship—all in God's great outdoors! In our symbolic picture of an ideal countryside, let religion stand out supreme. When the hearts of men rejoice because of God's presence in their midst, they show Him

gratitude by sacrifices of thanksgiving. So it appears to have been at Beth-shemesh, at least for a while. Every man present seems to have acted like a gentleman toward God.

3. *A change of feeling toward the Ark* (6:17–7:2). The verses about the golden tumors and the golden mice remind us that we are looking at a crude and backward people. Some of their ideas about religion seem to us disgusting. Unfortunately, such folk abound in every land today, not least in our own.[1] Some of our underprivileged citizens might not have difficulty in understanding the Hebrew narrative. They would say that it points to an attack of piles among townspeople, and a plague of mice among their country cousins. What concerns us now is the irreverence of the people at Beth-shemesh.

Because of that irreverence the Lord is said to have slain either seventy men or fifty thousand and seventy. The larger number must have crept into the text. After having twice visited the ruins of ancient Beth-shemesh, I can testify that a loss there of seventy men all at once would have proved staggering. Archaeological explorations show that Beth-shemesh could never have been more than a village. For a similar example, think of Oberammergau. Because of a plague in 1633 that hamlet suffered the loss of eighty persons out of six hundred. After a lapse of more than three hundred years the Bavarian village still commemorates that devastating plague. Fortunately, all the exercises at Oberammergau have taken the form of religion.

The death of the men at Beth-shemesh raises questions that none of us can answer. They have to do with the ways of God. Such problems keep rising throughout the course of Hebrew history. They emerge in New Testament days as well as in modern times. For instance, who can explain or justify the death and the immediate burial of Ananias and of his wife Sapphira?[2]

[1] See Frederick M. Davenport, *Primitive Traits in Religious Revivals,* Macmillan, 1910; also John Steinbeck's novel, *Of Mice and Men,* Viking, 1937.
[2] Acts 5:1-11.

How do we account for God's part in the plague at Oberammergau, and a little later over at the City of London? In the face of such incontrovertible facts, who but a Milton would attempt to

> assert Eternal Providence,
> And justify the ways of God to men?

With relief we turn away from grief-stricken Beth-shemesh. We can find satisfaction in looking at the men from Kiriathjearim. Incidentally, we note that they are said to have fetched the Ark up from Beth-shemesh. We remember that the reputed site of the former place towers above the ruins of the other "city" by almost a thousand feet. However we explain the fact, we who study the Old Testament have never found there a single geographical error.[3] On the contrary, any person who has attempted to lecture about a trip to Palestine will testify that his talk has been full of slips. In fact, he is tempted to make a pun out of that word "trip."

More vital than any geographical exactitude is the fact that the Ark rested in a farmer's home for twenty years. To that household the visible symbol of God's presence brought rich and abiding blessings. All the while where was King Saul? Why did he not see the wisdom of setting up the Ark in some strategic center? As soon as David took control he led to the selection of a national capital. There he established the Ark. From time to time, as other activities permitted, he began to make ready for the erection of a permanent temple. There he wished the Ark to repose as the visible token of God's presence among His chosen people. In terms of today, the life and the work of the nation ought to center round the Church of the Living God.

Do we appreciate the importance of having a church edifice

[3] See George Adam Smith, *The Historical Geography of the Holy Land*, rev. ed., Harper, 1932.

at the heart of every community? All of us may have grown up in neighborhoods which felt the influence of such local sanctuaries. If we had been born in certain districts of the West, or of Canada, as children we might have worshiped with our parents in all sorts of unseemly places. To such districts of Canada in the olden days went a strong man of God who became the builder of many rural churches. In pleading with pioneers to give money for a new church he insisted that such an edifice would impart to the work of the Lord both "visibility and permanence." [4]

As we glance back over this unpromising chapter in First Samuel let each of us make this resolve: By the grace of God I shall not rest until every community in our land, as well as across the sea, enjoys the blessings that flow from the sanctuary of God. Such an ideal calls for evangelism at home and for missions abroad.

[4] See Charles W. Gordon (Ralph Connor), *The Life of James Robertson*, Revell, 1908.

CHAPTER 7

THE CALL FOR A NATIONAL REVIVAL

1 Samuel 7:3-17

AT LAST WE ARRIVE AT ANOTHER OASIS. AFTER JOURNEYING THROUGH
a dry and thirsty land we come to the facts about Samuel. Under
his leadership the work of rebuilding the nation has begun.
For a score of years the Ark of God has been resting in a
farmer's house. Imagine a nation trying to get along without
God for twenty years! Yet it seems to have been so in various
parts of the world during our own times. Think especially of the
two decades prior to World War II. Is it not time that God
should begin to have His way, time for a national revival? [1]

A revival in our land! If any reader dislikes the term, let him
substitute some other. Whatever the title, Old Testament history
often tells about a season of quickening after a period of declen-
sion. Each time the course of events differed from that in other
revivals. A few factors, however, remained more or less constant.
These will emerge in the present chapter. All of them have to do
with God's way of using a strong leader. In terms of today
such a leader stands out as mighty in preaching, in prayer, and
in pastoral work. When such a minister comes into a community,
watch for the beginning of a revival!

1. *The word of the Lord through preaching* (vv. 3-4). Even
with the present meager report, the "sermon" by Samuel impresses the reader by its power. That resides partly in the verbs.
The dominant call to action rings out at the very start. "Return!"

[1] See Charles G. Finney, *Lectures on Revivals of Religion* (Revell, 1868), chap.
i-ii.

"Return unto the Lord with all your heart!" That sounds like the modern phrase "This business of being converted." But the Hebrew verb suggests more of good news from God. In much the same bold fashion Isaiah speaks from the heart of a mighty evangelistic chapter: "Seek ye the Lord while he may be found; call ye upon him while he is near: let the wicked forsake his way, and the unrighteous man his thoughts; and let him return unto the Lord, and he will have mercy upon him; and to our God, for he will abundantly pardon." [2]

After this positive appeal comes a negative command: "Put away the foreign gods." Whenever people return unto the God of their fathers the penitent sons relinquish every substitute for the Almighty. Much the same call for reformation, as well as repentance, issues from the opening chapter of Isaiah. After a terrific arraignment of the people's sins, the prophet sounds the wooing note: "Wash you, make you clean; put away the evil of your doings from before mine eyes; cease to do evil; learn to do well." [3] Then follows the assurance of pardon, of cleansing, and of peace. In our own day, likewise, the proclamation of judgment leads up to the offer of mercy.

Once again Samuel strikes a positive note: "Direct your hearts unto the Lord." In the Hebrew Bible this word "heart" refers to all that is within a man. The verb "direct" eludes attempts at definition. In general it signifies to do all in human power. The same term appears in the forefront of an Old Testament verse about a teaching minister: "Ezra had set his heart to seek the law of the Lord, and to do it, and to teach in Israel statutes and ordinances." [4] Whatever the rendering of the verb, the meaning stands out clear and strong. When people determine to get right with God, they find Him waiting to meet them with loving-kindness and tender mercy.

[2] Isa. 55:6-7.
[3] Isa. 1:16-17a.
[4] Ezra 7:10.

"And serve him only." Here again the prophet sounds the call for action. This time he summons the people to do the will of God. The ideal servants of our King belong to Him in body, mind, and soul. They do only what pleases Him. They perform every duty, and they do it well, not because they must, but because they can. They serve Him, and Him alone, not with the spirit of slaves, but with the gladness of sons. As a rule their service begins with public worship at the sanctuary. Then the spirit of practical devotion enters into all of life. If it proves difficult to define such loving service, the reason may be that it never becomes a matter of formal rules. In God the children of His heart live and move and have their being. They find that His "service is perfect freedom."

Last of all comes the promise of deliverance. Thus the messenger of God has spoken to the conscience and the will. He has called on the people to repent and to get right with God. On this basis he now brings the assurance of victory over the Philistines. How or when the promised triumph will come, he does not venture to predict. Perhaps he does not know, at least not yet. Nevertheless, he declares the will of God, and he holds out promises of mercy. How could Samuel feel so sure of his good news? Because he lived close to the heart of God. Thus he entered into the counsels of the Most High. Would that every local church had such a herald now! [5]

2. *The summons to united prayer* (vv. 5-9). Here at last we behold the nation on its knees. The assembly has convened at Mizpah. That seems to have been a mountain five miles northwest of Jerusalem. There the people prostrate themselves before the Lord. As a token of heart contrition they pour out water on the ground. They likewise confess their sins. They implore Samuel to pray for them, that they may get right with God.

[5] For a theory of prophetic preaching, turn to Henry H. Farmer, *The Servant of the Word*, Scribner, 1942.

How much of their distress springs from sorrow for sin, and how much from dread of the invading foe, who can tell? Neither kind of feeling seems to us unworthy. Whatever has driven them to their knees, that is where we behold them now. Watch how they shiver as they lie prostrate before the God whom they have long ignored. Since they know not how to pray, they need an intercessor.

"Cease not to cry unto the Lord our God for us, that he will save us." A short while ago these same people were putting their trust in the Ark: "It will save us!" Now they have begun to rely upon God. When they looked to the Ark for deliverance, they met with defeat. Now they follow a leader who assures them of victory if they turn to God with all their hearts. Still they seem not to know that Samuel has been praying for them even while they have not dreamed of asking for his intercession. Why do they not understand that his chief work on earth is to plead for those who cannot pray for themselves?

Thus we learn what it means for a nation to fall on its knees before God. Such a revival calls for a leader who summons the people to bow down and confess their sins. The movement also demands followers who will respond with all their hearts. However inarticulate their cries to the throne of grace, the suppliants must feel a strong desire to pray. In the case of Samuel one thing more seems to have been needful. On behalf of the waiting people he offered a sacrifice in the form of a burnt offering. Thus he signified their dedication to the service of God and their eagerness for His blessing. After the burnt offering the man of prayer cried unto the Lord for Israel. Then the answer came from the One who had long been waiting to bless His rebellious people. Is there no need of such a revival now?

3. *The deliverance from above* (vv. 10-11). The victory over the Philistines seems to have come where they had previously met with defeat. Then they had trusted in the symbol, and they

had found that it could not save. At last they looked up to God, and they did not look in vain. Even while they were engaging in worship, lying prone before the Lord, the hosts of the Philistines came sweeping on for the attack. Doubtless they expected to see the former weaklings flee without a fight. But those invading hosts failed to reckon with the Hebrew God. How could they know that He was standing beneath the shadows, keeping watch over His own? Had He not promised to deliver His imperiled children? Yea, verily, but who among friend or foe could have foretold how He would intervene?

"The Lord thundered with a great thunder." During the summer season it almost never thunders in the Holy Land. The driest period of all the year comes in the summer, which used to be the favorite time for engaging in war. Since the Philistines were discomfited and put to flight by the thunder, they must have been taken unawares. Hence we judge that the Lord "sent forth His voice" at a time of the year when everyone had a right to look for sunny skies, with never a storm. Some such facts may have led William Cowper to sing:

> God moves in a mysterious way
> His wonders to perform;
> He plants His footsteps in the sea,
> And rides upon the storm.

> Ye fearful saints, fresh courage take;
> The clouds ye so much dread
> Are big with mercy, and shall break
> In blessings on your head.

Is it proper to speak of such an event as a miracle? To be accurate, perhaps not. The Lord God simply employed what we call "the known laws of nature." Even so, He gave a signal demonstration of His overruling providence. That means, in part,

His way of looking out for His children and of making all things work together for their good. In other words, God set Himself to bring about the deliverance of His people. As soon as He saw that their hearts were ready He caused the invading hosts to become weak as water. Thus He accomplished for His people what they could never have begun to do for themselves. Is He not able to do for us now far more than we dare to ask or think?

4. *The erection of a memorial* (vv. 12-14). To those simple-hearted people a visible memorial would serve as a constant reminder of God's redeeming power. The name "Ebenezer," or "The Stone of Help," would tell them day after day that the One who had set them free from their enemies desired to keep on being their God. That silent symbol would lead them to think of God in terms of yesterday, today, and tomorrow. The stone of remembrance called for gratitude because of God's mercies in the past, for assurance because of His protection in the present, and for hope because of His promises for the future. From everlasting to everlasting He alone can be our God. As such He is ever near to His children. He is tender to sympathize and mighty to save:

> Our God, our Help in ages past,
> Our Hope for years to come,
> Our Shelter from the stormy blast,
> And our eternal Home.

Such a memorial exerts a stabilizing power over the hearts of God's children. Much the same feeling of gratitude must have led the fathers in Boston to select the motto of the newborn city: *Sicut patribus, sit Deus nobis.* That inscription on the seal of the city has led someone to remark: "If God is to be with us as He was with the fathers, we must be to God as the fathers were to Him." They proved their loyalty by putting near the center of every community a stately Colonial edifice. Unfortunately, they had a habit of naming the structure The First Church, or else The Second. Would it not have been more modest, and more meaningful, to have adopted such a title as Ebenezer?

5. *The pastor on a circuit* (vv. 15-17). The closing verses of the chapter introduce us to Samuel as a sort of circuit rider. Naturally his duties as a "judge" differed from the arduous labors of Francis Asbury. Even so, the Hebrew man of God must have stood out as the chief representative of religion in all that mountain area north of Jerusalem. To the present hour what rural district does not need such a man as Samuel who is ready and able to interpret the will of God for changing days? From time to time the leader serves as the public spokesman of the Most High. Whenever the opportunity arises, the interpreter stands forth to proclaim the truth. Like a shepherd he moves in and out among the flock. Thus he serves as friend, counselor, and guide. If every community in our land enjoyed the spiritual leadership of a pastor like Samuel, we might witness a national revival of religion.

Spiritually, we face the need of rebuilding our own nation and of helping to reclaim vast areas of "scorched earth" beyond the seven seas. In what mood shall we undertake to do our share in this work of spiritual reconstruction? Why should we not claim as our own the words that Charles G. Finney put at the forefront of his *Lectures on Revivals of Religion?*—"O Lord, revive thy work in the midst of the years, in the midst of the years make known; in wrath remember mercy." [6]

Let us therefore give special heed to the training of ministers for tomorrow. Under God, we must leave in their hands the welfare of our world. Again and again let us sing together that hymn of yesterday, "God of the Prophets, Bless the Prophets' Sons":

[6] Hab. 3:2*b* (A.V.).

THE CALL FOR A NATIONAL REVIVAL

Anoint them prophets! Make their ears attent
  To Thy divinest speech; their hearts awake
To human need; their lips make eloquent
  To gird the right and every evil break.

Anoint them priests! Strong intercessors they
  For pardon, and for charity and peace!
O that with them might pass the world, astray,
  Into the dear Christ's life of sacrifice.[7]

[7] The Rev. Denis Workman, 1884.

CHAPTER 8

THE WRONG WAY TO SECURE A LEADER

I Samuel 8

ONCE AGAIN WE APPROACH A DIFFICULT PASSAGE. AS WITH THE LAST problem, this one concerns the will of God. In the days of Samuel the children of Israel were suffering for lack of a national leader. They must have longed for a man like Moses. And yet the Lord seems to have granted their request reluctantly. Before we discuss the situation further, let us remind ourselves of the facts.

1. *The presence of unworthy leaders* (vv. 1-3). The prophet Samuel had begun to grow old. Erelong he would have to lay down his portion of life's burdens. Like Eli, this other father had failed to rear the right sort of sons. For some reason unknown, Eli and Samuel seem to have had more influence almost everywhere else than at home. Worse still, each of those sires proposed to hand over the leadership of God's people to young sons totally unworthy of public trust. Instead of relegating his wayward scions to private life, Samuel actually designated them as his successors.

The sins of Samuel's sons resembled those of Eli's boys. The two sets of young fellows yielded to the lure of easy money. They even went out of their way to solicit bribes. Hence they made a travesty of public justice. And yet they stood among men as public representatives of the God whose name is the Holy One. All of this we must consider if we are to understand the action of the elders. They refused to let such wild young fellows become the official leaders of the nation. Those elders may have been thinking about the recent times under the Judges: "In those days there was no king in Israel: every man did that which was right in his own eyes."[1] What an indirect description of anarchy!

2. *The demand for a king* (vv. 4-9). The record shows the wrong way to secure something that is right. Those men properly desired a leader more worthy than either of Samuel's sons. But why did the elders demand "a king to judge us like all the nations"? Were not those neighboring peoples suffering under the rule of despots? Since the children of Israel served the Lord God of Hosts, why did they long to become like the nations that worshiped other gods? Hence it seems that improper motives may lead to desirable actions. If it were not so, we might have to dwell in a world even worse than ours of today.[2]

According to the biblical account, Samuel felt aggrieved. Perhaps he had hoped that added responsibilities would cause his wayward "boys" to settle down. More probably he had let fatherly love blind his eyes to the sons' excesses. Then, too, he must have been shocked to see the people turning to the customs of surrounding nations. Fortunately, before he tried to appraise their actions Samuel went to God in prayer. Through the years he had formed the habit of looking up for guidance in every hour of uncertainty or crisis. Sometimes, as here, the man of God discovers truth that he finds difficulty in accepting. But even in the face of that discovery Samuel did not flinch.

"They have not rejected thee," said the Lord, "but they have rejected me, that I should not be king over them." As often elsewhere in human history, God let the children of Israel have their way. Such a course involves "permission without sanction." In like manner, when young folk insist on going their own gait,

---

[1] Judg. 21:25; cf. Judg. 17:6.

[2] For a different interpretation of the facts see Pfeiffer, *Introduction to the Old Testament,* p. 360. Like other scholars, Professor Pfeiffer explains such difficulties on the basis of dual authorship, with two conflicting accounts.

despite all that godly parents can do to dissuade, the time comes when the young people must have their own way, whatever the cost. Such tragedies often spring from the desire to secure lofty ends through improper means. When shall we mortals humble ourselves and look to the Lord for guidance in living according to ideals that come from above?

3. *The wrong sort of national leader* (vv. 10-18). In the name of his God the prophet told the people what sort of tyrannical ruler they might expect. The faults that he pointed out have appeared in unworthy kings during almost every age of human history. For example, think of King Solomon, Louis XIV, or Louis XV. Unlike other historians, who dwell on the luxury and wantonness of life at the royal court, our sacred writer points out the tragic effects of tyranny upon the common people. Their sons and daughters suffer endless hardship. Because of the king's extravagance, oppression, and militarism, they become virtual serfs. In the end they cry out from tyranny to God. Are there no such scenes across the seven seas today?

We may conclude that people often secure as good a government as they deserve. In view of this fact, what should we do? Since we elect our own rulers, let us ask for guidance and restraint. Instead of doing our utmost to become like other powers, which have led the world into war after war, let us rather seek to know and do the will of the Lord. Not only is "every man's life a plan of God." He likewise has a program for each of His servant nations, including our own. If we had such interpreters and intercessors as Samuel, we could be guided into paths of honor and peace. So let us beseech the Lord our God to raise up a generation of pastors like unto Samuel.

Chapter 9

THE WILL OF GOD FOR A MAN'S CAREER

I Samuel 9

THE NINTH CHAPTER OF FIRST SAMUEL LEADS TO A STUDY OF THE Lord's will for a man's lifework. Needless to say, the question looms large at a time when the world has grown weary of war and has turned millions of young men back into the gentle paths of peace. As a matter of fact, the Lord guides every willing youth or maiden differently. Nevertheless, amid all the countless variations, a few general principles emerge. Some of these basic truths appear in the chapter we now study.

1. *A young man who is not expecting word from above* (vv. 1-4). Saul had gone forth in quest of his father's asses, which had strayed from home. Doubtless the young man had looked forward to a life of honorable toil back on the hills of home. When the Lord summoned Chrysostom to become a herald of the gospel he had set his heart on becoming a lawyer. Frederick W. Robertson had prepared for life service as a soldier. More than one of us present-day ministers used to dream of doing something else. The writer had planned to become a college professor of English. But when the summons arrives from the King of Kings, who would dare decline? Let us rather think of that masterful sermon by Horace Bushnell, "Every Man's Life a Plan of God." [1]

The young man called of God has already formed the habit of working hard. However humdrum and wearisome the task, he has set himself to do it well. When young Saul hies forth to

[1] In *The New Life* (sermons; London, 1869), pp. 1-15.

find his father's asses, the search continues until it meets with success. In like manner, when Joseph serves in the prison house, when David watches over the sheep, when Elisha busies himself with the oxen at the plow, in each case the future leader of men shows his fitness for advancement by fidelity to his prosaic task. For a later example think of Oliver Cromwell. Up until he had passed the age of forty he kept working day after day as the owner and tiller of a small farm. Then he turned to mighty exploits that taxed all his highly developed powers. For the supreme object lesson look at the earthly life of our Lord. In an age when other teachers of religion would not soil their hands with menial tasks, the Prince of Glory became the Carpenter of Nazareth.

2. *A young man consults with a wise friend of God* (vv. 5-10). The procedure of giving advice in a time of uncertainty has become known as "personal counseling." In the work of the parish minister the idea may call for a "pastor's hour." Whatever the plan, such friendly counseling is new only in name. Throughout the history of the Church every pastor called of God has engaged in a heart-to-heart ministry of man to man. So has every worthy chaplain, or missionary. This kind of personal counseling affords the most searching test of any clergyman's fitness to act as God's undershepherd.

The personal counselor needs to be a man of strong character as well as spotless reputation. In dealing with the weak and the sinful, the pastoral adviser needs to know the Word of God as well as the hearts of men. In helping a young fellow learn what to do with his life, the older man must have a wealth of practical wisdom. How else could he diagnose one case after another? With all his other gifts and graces, the counselor needs a high degree of intellectual power. Otherwise he might fail to solve various personal problems with all their perplexities. In brief, look at Samuel. Think of him as an ideal pastoral counselor.

THE WILL OF GOD FOR A MAN'S CAREER

"There is in this city a man of God, and he is a man that is held in honor; all that he saith cometh surely to pass." What a reputation for a minister to gain in his home town! When a young man in bewilderment finds such an older friend as Samuel, the light is almost sure to break. On the contrary, listen to Pascal. He wrote three hundred years ago, but his words sound a warning today: "Believe me, it takes no small effrontery to reach a helping hand to the struggling, to provide counsel for the uncertain, and hope for the discouraged, and new heart for the tired. These are, indeed, proud achievements if the thing works out. But the project grows ridiculous if it all comes to nothing."

3. *The young man tarries for a while in the house of prayer* (vv. 11-14). In guiding the young man to the sanctuary the Lord may use humble agents. With Saul, He employed maidservants on their way to draw water from the community well. In bringing about the healing of Naaman the leper, God used a captive maidservant as well as a man of the same lowly rank. Such an agent may know little about books. Nevertheless, the humblest servant may have at the tongue's end exactly the word that the bewildered young man needs to hear. How carefully our God looks after each of His children!

Why did Saul turn his face toward the sanctuary? Because that was where he expected to find Samuel. Even for such a human reason, it is good when a young man seeks the house of the Lord. There he will enter into the sort of atmosphere that will prepare his heart to receive truth from God. For this reason, if for no other, every local church ought to stand open seven days in the week. Ideally, someone like Samuel ought to be stationed there, ready to confer with any person who wishes to ascertain the will of God.[2]

[2] See Henry B. Wright, *The Will of God and a Man's Lifework,* Association Press, 1909.

73

4. *The young seeker begins to feel humble* (vv. 15-21). When Samuel unfolded before Saul's eyes something of what the Lord had in store for the farmer's son, the young man's response showed a commendable spirit of meekness. He felt unworthy. That need not seem strange. Was it not so with Moses at the burning bush, and with Gideon at the threshing floor? When has a strong man ever felt worthy of a new commission from his God?

Every pastor can recall examples of such reluctance. Every year the writer used to interview one man after another whom a committee wished to propose for church leadership. Never once did he confer with a worthy layman who felt good enough for a high spiritual office. Others felt entirely capable; they wondered why they were not invited. Two related facts stand out from those interviews: after much hesitation every one of those modest men accepted the opportunity for service; and, without exception, each lay officer performed his duties with something approaching distinction. What a privilege for a minister to be associated with God's noblest gentlemen!

5. *He waits for more light* (vv. 22-27). At first he may feel the temptation to rush back home and tell the loved ones about the new commission. That may be exactly what the appointee must not do. What right has Saul to inform others that he is destined to become king? Rather does he learn to keep his own counsel. He must likewise ascertain what personal adjustments he has to make. Such light comes best through the older friend who has already interpreted the will of the Lord.

The needful direction may also come through fellowship with other men. Well did mature Samuel know that the future king of Israel needed to become acquainted with the men whom he was afterward to lead. Hence the prophet arranged for Saul to be the guest of honor at a banquet. There he could keep his own counsel and still get to know the stalwart men who were later to become his followers and friends. Thus it appears that the will of the Lord calls for a vast deal of practical wisdom. Among other things, God makes provision that the new leader shall start out with the good will of his future followers.

In all these matters God seldom leaves a young man to wander alone. In any hour of bewilderment the youth can seek out a man of mature wisdom, somewhat like Samuel. For instance, take John Henry Jowett, who was later to become the foremost evangelical preacher of his time. Once while young he faced a difficult and delicate decision. Not knowing which way to turn or what to do, the young man went to an older minister named Berry. That man of God listened intently while young Jowett explained the situation. Then Dr. Berry led in prayer. As young Jowett made ready to leave, without having caught a gleam of light, the older man asked, "When must you decide?" Jowett answered, "Not later than next Friday at noon." "Very well," said Dr. Berry, "before Friday at noon the path of duty will become clear." So it proved. The light does not always break forth at once. But when the time comes for a man to act, if he has done his part, he will know. All of this takes for granted a heart right with God and a life attuned to His holy will. "If any man willeth to do His will, he shall know." [9]

What a lofty ideal this chapter sets before the parish minister, as well as the chaplain or the missionary! Whenever a young man comes in quest of practical advice, no matter how commonplace the problem, remember that he may be standing at the fork in life's roadway. Be ready to show concern like that of Samuel. Be ready, also, with the sort of skill that comes from having dealt with other friends in quest of expert aid. In the case of young Saul the friendly adviser needed to know that the father back at home had begun to feel far more anxious about his missing

[9] John 7:17. See F. W. Robertson, "Obedience the Organ of Spiritual Knowledge," in Sermons (Harper, n.d.), pp. 300-7; and Phillips Brooks, "The Illumination of Obedience," in Sermons (Dutton, 1910), V, 340-58.

son than about the stray asses. The counselor also needed to learn that the farmer's son had been chosen of God to become a king. All this may enter occasionally into "the romance of the ministry." [4]

To serve as a pastoral counselor, therefore, means to do for one person at a time what the man in the pulpit endeavors to do for a waiting throng. Whether it be in the study, facing a bewildered friend, or in the sanctuary, addressing a wistful multitude, the man of God needs to interpret human life today, in the light that comes from God.[5] In public or in private the minister will find it easier to make known the will of the Lord if he lives every day close to the heart of God.

From a different point of view a philosopher writes: "When I am in a practical perplexity, such as often arises in daily life, that friend can best advise me who helps me to ignore useless complications, to see simply and directly, to look at the central facts of my situation."[6] In the deepest matters of the soul how can the interpreter do all of that unless he follows the guidance of the Holy Spirit?

[4] See Raymond Calkins, *The Romance of the Ministry,* Pilgrim, 1944.

[5] See Blackwood, "The Value of a Pastor's Hour," chap. xxiv of *Pastoral Work,* Westminster, 1945.

[6] Josiah Royce, *The Philosophy of Loyalty* (Macmillan, 1908), p. 149.

CHAPTER 10

THE BEGINNING OF A MAN'S LIFEWORK

I Samuel 10

THE EFFECTIVENESS OF A MAN'S LIFEWORK DEPENDS LARGELY ON HOW he starts. King Saul's career began auspiciously. Even so, that did not insure his final success. In fact, anyone who takes delight in paradoxes can find them in the records about this leader of men. At present, however, we may close our eyes to the anticlimactic close of his career and think about the brightness of the beginning.

1. *A man should be certain about his call from God* (vv. 1-8). What else could have given young Saul such a feeling of security as did the ceremony that preceded the beginning of his active career? When the chief living representative of the Most High God poured anointing oil on the head of young Saul, what did the action symbolize? Nothing less than personal enduement by the Holy Spirit for service among men. "The Lord hath anointed thee to be prince over his inheritance." The word translated "prince," or "leader," stands out strongly in the Hebrew. The same term appears in Isaiah 55:4: "I have given him for a witness to the peoples, *a leader* and commander to the peoples."

Once again the historian shows his mastery of light and shadow. He excels in the use of contrast. He has been recounting the old prophet's words about the kingship. Then the record turns to the young man's father. He "hath left off caring for the asses, and is anxious for you, saying, What shall I do for my son?" What a touching picture of paternal love! Others may think of Saul as the future monarch. To his father back at home the young fellow is only a lad to be shielded from life's rough blasts! What a text for a Father's Day sermon! [1] These words might even help one bring religion into the main talk at a Father-and-Son Banquet. Does not many a strong man of middle age or beyond cease to live mainly for himself and think much about his children, especially the eldest son?

The most important part of the Bible paragraph under consideration has to do with Saul's receiving the power of the Holy Spirit. Thus he became gifted as a public speaker. He was even transformed into "another man." Here again the record leads into mystery. This much, however, we know: up to the present hour the young man has shown none of the unseemly traits that will mark him when he becomes leader of the nation. In fact, as long as he accepts and follows the "inner light," which some of us know as the guidance of the Holy Spirit, the new king proves to be mighty in word and deed. At certain hours of crisis he becomes practically invincible. Surely this is what every leader of men ought to seek and find—the power of the Holy Spirit for service.

Still the ceremony seems to have been incomplete. The newly anointed ruler needed to tarry with the man of God for seven days. Together they were to engage in definite acts of worship. Their special sacrifices consisted of burnt offerings and peace offerings. In terms of our day, those ceremonial acts symbolized complete dedication to God and heartfelt rendering of thanks. Who can wonder that the new work started out on a lofty plane and then moved forward with irresistible force? In fact, as long as the king enjoyed the presence and the counsel of Samuel, the new regime met with the blessing of God and the favor of men. All because of one man's leadership, that of God's minister.

In the British House of Commons sixty years ago Joseph

[1] See Blackwood, "Observing Special Days," chap. ii of *Planning a Year's Pulpit Work*, Abingdon-Cokesbury, 1942.

Chamberlain stood out above his fellows. One day in a spirited debate he was taunted with representing a constituency of a single person. That one man proved to be Robert William Dale, a Nonconformist pastor in Birmingham. Instead of resenting the charge, Chamberlain thanked his critic, and then remarked that no one could wish for a nobler constituency. How much more could King Saul have rejoiced in carrying out the will of God as made known through the prophet Samuel! Why should not every monarch have near at hand such a wise interpreter of God's will for the nation?

2. *A man needs to be careful about what he does first* (vv. 9-13). When a leader has been filled with the Spirit of Light, he determines to make the most of all his God-given powers. He begins to use them for the good of his fellow men. That must have held true with King Saul. The record states that "God gave him another heart." In the Hebrew this term "gave" carries a sense of power. Often the word means "to turn." The same verb appears in Psalm 66:6, which refers to the crossing of the Red Sea: "He turned the sea into dry land." In other words, as we often say, the young man "found himself."

Hence he began to speak out boldly as the public representative of the Almighty. When the Book says that the king prophesied, there need be no reference to the use of prediction. Surely that entered into the lifework of such a seer as Isaiah. But with King Saul the prophesying doubtless moved on a lower level. He must have confined himself to the demands of the hour. Even so, he took his place among the seers: "Is Saul also among the prophets?" Not according to our customary way of reckoning! But do we not know that the leader of strong men must have the ability to stand up and speak out? That, Saul could do most acceptably, as long as he forgot himself. Hence he could throw all his energies into doing the will of God. What an auspicious beginning for a man's lifework!

3. *A young man needs to keep his own counsel* (vv. 14-16). Ability to refrain from divulging secrets constitutes no small part of a man's equipment for service. Young Saul met the test. When his uncle inquired about the expedition, which had been unduly prolonged, the nephew explained about the finding of the asses, but not about the news of the kingship. With no semblence of duplicity, he told the truth but not the whole truth. Some such practical wisdom led former President Coolidge to remark that his custom of remaining silent had never once involved him in difficulty. Still more recently, during World War II, when an officious chaplain asked his colonel about the military plans for the coming night, the commanding officer inquired, "Can you keep a secret?" "Yes, sir!" "So can I!" That may have been one reason why he became a colonel!

Ability to keep a secret shows self-control. The importance of such poise appears in a brilliant address by Sir William Osler, M.D.[2] During World War I he became known over in England as "The Consoler-General of the British Army." Out of his rich and varied experience he spoke to other physicians about the call for equanimity. "There are only two sorts of doctors: those who practice with their brains, and those who practice with their tongues." Dr. Osler insisted that the physician who betrayed indecision in ordinary affairs, and became flustered in an emergency, must have mistaken his calling. What a lesson for the young minister, or any other leader of men!

This line of thought suggests a practical question. How can a young leader be friendly and tactful, as well as truthful and sincere, without telling too much, and without seeming two-faced? Whatever the secret, many a young minister has done so, and that from the beginning of his lifework. Such ability comes from God, not least through the act of ordination. In the anointing of the Hebrew priest, sacrificial blood was applied to

[2] See his *Aequanimitas* (4th impression, London, 1920), pp. 4, 131.

the tip of the right ear, the thumb of the right hand, and the great toe of the right foot.[3] What does all this mean in terms of today? That the young pastor needs the blessing of God in the use of his hearing, in his handiwork, and in all his pastoral ministry. As for his tongue, that does not here enter into the equation. The pastor serves best when he listens eagerly and talks little. This kind of self-control appeared in King Saul, at least for a while. Afterward, when he lost his equanimity, he likewise relinquished his power.

4. *Be sure to receive authority from men* (vv. 17-24). At this stage the action shifts again to Mizpah. That seems to have been the prophet's first choice as the scene of a religious ceremony.[4] There he addressed the children of Israel. After a survey of their history he led up to a disclosure about the new king. Thus the prophet associated the new regime with faith in the God of their fathers. The aging seer also provided a keynote for the ceremony of the day. In substance he said to the waiting throng: "Behold your King! Long live the King! He comes from God!"

Without any intention of doing so, the young man supplied the antithesis. "When they sought him, he could not be found." What welcome modesty! Evidently the office sought the man. Shortly thereafter the people found Saul hidden among the baggage. Such a spirit of self-effacement might conceivably be carried too far. Still it speaks well for a young man when he hesitates about accepting tasks beyond his conscious powers. Can you wonder that the young king felt as weak as water, and that the prophet looked on him with satisfaction? "See ye him whom the Lord hath chosen, that there is none like him among all the people?" Then the multitude cried out, "Long live the king!"

Thus we behold "a man born to be king." We likewise witness a noble way of introducing a new leader. Was ever such a

[3] Lev. 8:23.
[4] Cf. I Sam. 7:5.

delicate undertaking carried out with more skill and tact? Throughout the entire proceedings both the older man and the younger one appeared at their best. Each of them dared simply to be himself. By bluntness in presenting the new monarch, without first preparing the hearts of the people, Samuel might have made it hard for the incoming ruler to win their allegiance. By unseemly haste in grasping powers never before granted to any Hebrew leader, young Saul might have antagonized the people who were to become his followers and friends. Fortunately, no untoward actions marred that glorious day. In fact, as long as Saul enjoyed the presence and the counsel of Samuel, the young king avoided every pitfall.

5. *The wise leader enlists a band of loyal followers* (vv. 25-27). In terms of our day, the wise leader as soon as possible captures the imagination of his followers. At first he may suggest nothing spectacular. Saul did not immediately launch a whirlwind campaign against the Philistines. He was not prepared for any advance movement and neither were the people. For much the same reason, during World War II General Bernard Montgomery did not begin his work in North Africa by hurling all his forces against those of General Rommel. Wisely the English commander waited until all was ready. Then he went on to triumph. Meantime he had gained the confidence of his officers and men. Later when a friend asked how he had felt before the most critical hour, Montgomery calmly replied: "I am never anxious when I fight my battles. If I am anxious I don't fight them. I wait until I am ready."

Such a leader inspires loyalty in his followers. When young Saul departed from the scene of his reception as king, "there went with him the host, whose hearts God had touched." What an ideal! A ruler set apart by the ministering servant of God, and a people whose hearts God has filled with a desire to follow their leader! Men like to be led. If they trust the man whom they should follow, they will go with him unto death. This is what we understand by loyalty. It works both ways: as long as the king remains loyal to his God, the people continue loyal to their king. In this spirit President Harry S. Truman said in closing his first address to the nation: "I ask only to be a good and faithful servant of my Lord and my people." [5]

On the other hand, a worthy leader must expect opposition. "Certain worthless fellows said, How shall this man save us?" Once again we note the author's skill in the use of contrast. First he shows the good, and then the bad. Over against the king, with a host of followers whose hearts God has touched, behold a smaller group of "willful men." Their main business in life appears to be finding fault. Though not themselves engaged in any forward movement, they strive to prevent others from doing the will of God. Wise is the leader who foresees such tactics and then does not swerve from his own path of duty. Hence the chapter closes with the pregnant saying "He held his peace." Another proof of the new king's equanimity!

"Silence may be eloquence, and speak thy worth above the power of words." So said wise old Sir Thomas Browne. Let every would-be leader pay careful heed. When do-nothing onlookers begin to sneer at the "young upstart," what should he say in self-defense? Nothing! Wise is the leader who early forms the habit of not attempting to justify himself or his actions. He should know that in time they will speak for themselves. Meanwhile he must wait until he has sized up the situation. Gladly should he welcome the support of everyone who stands ready to help. Modestly should he accept whatever comes in the way of mud and stones. A wise leader learns much from his fiercest critics. In our own early history was it not so with George Washington? In fact, young Saul appears to have been more

[5] Apr. 16, 1945. He had just voiced part of Solomon's Prayer, I Kings 3:9a.

than a little like Washington when he left Mount Vernon to lead the Colonies out toward freedom.

What an auspicious start for young King Saul! And yet he has merely begun. Before many years have gone by he will have displayed an increasing number of shortcomings and perversities, leading him to the most humiliating failures and defeats. What a series of danger signals for a young man called of God to guide His people, especially in days of rebuilding!

CHAPTER 11

THE ETHICS OF DEFENSIVE WARFARE

I Samuel 11

WE COME TO A QUESTION ABOUT WHICH THE WISEST AND THE BEST of men differ, sometimes sharply. Is it ever right or needful for a country to engage in a defensive war? Especially in our days of so-called peace, the issue may have no place in the pulpit. Listen to Arthur John Gossip, of Glasgow, addressing young students of theology: "It is seldom that a man has the right to lay it down in the pulpit that on a debatable question of the day he has the mind of Christ, and that whoso differs from him parts with the Master. . . . Gentlemen, stick to your own job." [1]

But what if the question follows a man into the study, or the conference room? No self-respecting clergyman will dare to dodge the issue there. This is one of several ways in which it may come: a young soldier consults his pastor about a case of right or wrong. He has recently come back from Okinawa, or from Germany. His nerves have given way. He cannot sleep at night or toil by day. At last, near the brink of the abyss, he calls on the minister of the home church. In the study the conscience-stricken soldier cries out, "Padre, the Good Book says, 'Thou shalt not kill.' Did I do wrong when I went to war, and slew my fellow men?"

Whether that question ever comes out or not, every minister needs to know his answer. Down in his heart does he look on our millions of returning soldiers and sailors as heroes worthy of praise, or as murderers to be condemned? For each of them, to

[1] *In Christ's Stead* (Warrack Lectures; Doran, 1925), p. 36.

engage in World War II must have been either right or wrong.[2] What is your answer? Instead of trying to deal with the issue abstractly, or even pontifically, let us examine a case from life. The incursion of the Ammonites into Israel raises many of the problems that have emerged in World War II. The smallness of the ancient arena of warfare may help us to see the facts clearly.

1. *The conditions that lead to a defensive war* (vv. 1-5). Think of the Ammonites as a fierce and bloodthirsty host, like the Japanese at Pearl Harbor or Corregidor. Watch those ancient invaders as they prepare to swoop down on the defenseless people of Gilead, a sparsely settled grazing district east of the Jordan. Take for granted that the incursion has been unprovoked. That seems to have been the case with most of the strife recorded in First and Second Samuel. Indeed, certain scholars insist that King David never engaged in any war except one of defense. At present, however, we need not examine such claims. We are looking at a single case.

The incoming hosts of the Ammonites surely outnumbered the people on the hills of Gilead. The enemy was far better equipped. Hence the invaders began to make insolent and inhuman demands. Thus they responded to the well-known policy of "appeasement." How could feeble farmers hope to arrange for a just and lasting peace with bloodthirsty tigers? The "modest proposal" of the enemy simply consisted in demanding that every man of Gilead forfeit his right eye! If that had been done, the other eye also might have been gouged out. Then the most valiant trooper would have been as helpless as Samson, "blind in Gaza."

Such an account may sound extreme. If so, think of the way the Japanese looted city after city in China, and then defiled the bodies of countless girls. Those warriors from Nippon likewise

[2] See Edwyn R. Bevan, *Christians in a World at War* (London, 1940), especially chap. viii, "Pacifism."

perpetrated unspeakable outrages against our armed forces and our captive soldiers. So did the Germans commit atrocities unspeakable. Of course, we of the English-speaking world have not always treated either of those powers with justice and mercy. Without detracting at all from the enormity of their guilt, we can think more objectively about Japan in China. What lover of peace can condemn Father Chisholm, in *The Keys of the Kingdom,* for his noble part in a war of defense? A pacifist at heart, as most of us are, that mission worker in China took up arms and used them to succor native Christians. Such is the issue about which wise and good men differ. Is it ever right or needful to engage in a purely defensive war?

2. *The spirit that leads to a defensive war* (vv. 6-11). As a rule, international strife grows out of motives and impulses bred and nurtured in hell. "Whence come wars and whence come fightings among you? come they not hence, even of your pleasures that war in your members?"[3] Never has our long-suffering earth witnessed carnage that did not issue from forces satanic. On a different level the same holds true of divorce. In an ideal world young men would not learn war any more, and young women would never demand divorce. But what had these ideals to do with poor old China? What had she done to provoke the inrush of countless warriors from the Flowery Kingdom? As with the wife of a drunken brute, should our dear old friend in the Far East have calmly submitted to unspeakable brutality and degradation? Should not China rather have done her utmost to rescue her outraged daughters?

Now let us turn to our case from Samuel. "The Spirit of God came mightily upon Saul, ... and his anger was kindled greatly." These words from the Bible lead to the heart of our problem.[4]

[3] James 4:1.
[4] See Umphrey Lee, *The Historic Church and Modern Pacifism,* Abingdon-Cokesbury, 1943.

Did that infuriated leader carry out the will of God, or of Satan? Before you attempt to formulate a reply, look again at the facts. Note how the enraged king aroused the men of Israel to action. "The dread of the Lord fell on the people, and they came out as one man." However rashly, they entered into that contest expecting to win. Hence they triumphed, through powers of which they had never dreamed. Partly by valor, more through strategy, they repelled the bloodthirsty invaders.

For another ancient example of defensive strife, turn to the fourteenth chapter of Genesis. Note that Abram did nothing to provoke the attack by five kings from the East. He might well have submitted to the loss of his cattle and sheep. But when he learned that the invaders had carried away his nephew Lot, the old lover of peace assembled his young men of war, pursued the homeward-bound foes, and rescued their captives. By way of recompense Abram demanded nothing for himself and his troops except what they had eaten along the route of battle. Who will contend that Abram did wrong? Indeed, who could have defended him if he had not taken up arms to deliver that captive?

> 'Tis man's perdition to be safe,
> When for the truth he ought to die.

Such a reading of the facts may seem cruel and revengeful. If so, remember that we are looking back upon "Israel's Iron Age."[5] Not even there can we discover atrocities and outrages so nearly demonic as those we followed in recent years through the *New York Times*. Reluctantly many of us concluded that a defensive war, like that of China, had become a tragic necessity. We must look upon Madame Chiang Kai-shek as carrying out the will of God when she demanded heroic resistance by force of arms. All the while we hope that world missions will some day lead to the triumph of righteousness and the reign of peace.

[5] See Marcus Dods, *Israel's Iron Age* (Doran, n.d.), a helpful book about the era of the Judges.

For the same kind of masculine religion turn to Frederick W. Robertson, perhaps the most influential preacher thus far in the English-speaking world. At heart a soldier, he schooled himself to restrain his ire. However, "the indignation with which he heard of a base act was so intense that it rendered him sleepless. His wrath was terrible, and it did not evaporate in words. But it was Christlike indignation. . . . 'I have seen him,' writes one of his friends, 'grain his teeth and clench his fist when passing a man, who, he knew, was bent on destroying an innocent girl.' 'My blood,' he himself writes, after a conversation on the wrongs of women, 'was running liquid fire.' "[6]

The very same spirit, on a larger scale, has led many a righteous man to believe in a war of defense. Who will say that saintly soldiers have always been mistaken in their attitude toward strife among the nations? They have felt a sense of guidance by the Spirit of God. However numerous the exceptions, and however deplorable the conclusion, shall we not grant that occasionally it becomes an inevitable duty to take up arms and repel an invading foe who would torture and enslave a submissive people?

2. *The peace that follows a defensive war* (vv. 12-13). The brief record in Samuel makes no mention of indemnities or reprisals. The spirit of revenge would have led the victors to gouge out the right eye of every Ammonite warrior taken captive. Perhaps the conquerors found it hard to catch the fleeing foes. Whatever the reason, the war stopped when the invasion ceased. In like manner, the triumphant leader showed no desire to wreak vengeance on do-nothing critics at home. His spirit seems to have been that of gratitude to God for deliverance from a fate worse than death, and of desire for peace with foes who had tasted the horrors of war. If such a spirit of conciliation had followed the death of Lincoln in April, 1865, and the Armistice in November,

---

[6] Stopford A. Brooke, *Life and Letters of Fred. W. Robertson* (London, 1873), I, 196-97.

1918, we might now enjoy more of peace and good will here at home, as well as across the sea. In those two cases the years of "reconstruction" seem to have wrought far more lasting injuries than the days of bloody strife.[7] Will the same prove true about today?

For a living example of magnanimity after a war, turn to the now famous address by Madame Chiang Kai-shek at Madison Square Garden. The excerpt below includes items that have seldom been quoted:

We live in the present, we dream of the future, but we learn eternal truths from the past. . . . There must be no bitterness in the reconstructed world. No matter what we have undergone and suffered, we must try to forgive those who injured us, and remember only the lesson gained thereby. . . . Selfishness and complacency in the past have made us pay dearly in terms of human misery and suffering. While it may be difficult for us not to feel bitterness for the injuries we have suffered at the hands of the aggressors, let us remember that recrimination and hatred will lead us nowhere.[8]

4. *The revival that may follow a war* (vv. 14-15). After the coming of peace the Israelites assembled at one of their shrines. There they "renewed" the Kingdom. Once again they solemnly ratified the covenant made with their king in the presence of God. Anew they dedicated the government to the King of Kings. They showed their gratitude to the Most High by making sacrificial thank offerings. In short, they enjoyed what we call a revival of religion. Is not Old Testament history largely the record of national fallings away from the faith of the fathers and periodic revivals in the form of turning to God? What else do we need so much today, here in our homeland as well as throughout the world?

[7] See Claude G. Bowers, *The Tragic Era: The Revolution After Lincoln*, Houghton, Mifflin, 1929.

[8] In *Vital Speeches of the Day*, Mar. 15, 1943.

THE ETHICS OF DEFENSIVE WARFARE

Many good folk at home and abroad have dreaded the advent of peace. They have wondered how our war-weary world could endure the letdown that must ensue after contending hosts have laid aside their arms. Surely the peoples of earth still need the grace of God as much as they did when battles raged. If we as a world are to escape from an aftermath of calamity and chaos, destruction and death, we must have a far-reaching revival of the religion that consists in righteousness, peace, and joy in the Holy Ghost, all in the spirit of Christ and His Cross.

Someone may question the use of the word "revival." Very well, let Woodrow Wilson voice the idea in other terms. Under the heading "The Road Away from Revolution" he sent forth to the people of the United States his swan song. Almost five years after the end of World War I he wrote:

Our civilization cannot survive materially unless it is redeemed spiritually. It can be saved only by being permeated with the Spirit of Christ, and being made free and happy by the practices which spring out of that Spirit. Only thus can discontent be driven out and all the shadows lifted. . . . Here is the final challenge to our churches, . . . to everyone who fears God or loves his country. Shall we not all earnestly coöperate to bring in the new day? [9]

Like Madame Chiang Kai-shek, Woodrow Wilson loved peace more than anything else save honor. We who revere his memory share his horror of war. Nevertheless many of us believe with him that entrance into conflict sometimes becomes a solemn duty to God. As for the Friends, or Quakers, we cherish for them the highest regard. We feel that if they could enter more largely into the counsels of the nations the hope for days ahead would be far more bright. Surely we ought never to quarrel with friends and neighbors who sincerely love and serve the God of peace. The fact remains that when eleven millions of our choicest young

[9] *The Atlantic Monthly*, August, 1923.

men enrolled for battle beneath the flag, either they did right or they did wrong. There can be no neutral ground.

This problem led to an absorbing debate a few summers ago at Chautauqua. Two able clergymen took opposing sides. When the time came for questions from the floor, someone asked Reinhold Niebuhr, one of the debaters: "Is it true that in certain circles today 40 per cent of our clergymen think it wrong to engage in defensive war?"

"Yes," was the answer, "in some quarters that would be a fair estimate."

"Dr. Niebuhr, what do you think of such a situation?"

At once came the reply: "Thank God for our laymen!"

Rightly or wrongly, the vast majority of our laymen accepted our entrance into World War II as a tragic necessity. They looked upon the giving up of their sons as a duty. These fathers and mothers reasoned that if our sons had not gone forth to battle our statesmen could never have concluded any kind of peace with Germany or Japan. All of that terrible alternative must lie in the misty realms of conjecture. But there ought to be nothing hazy about the minister's attitude toward any young man who has returned from war with blood on his hands and a question on his lips. Somehow or other, answer that question so as to bring him peace of heart.

At the present writing the skies look dark. In days to come they may grow darker. The release of the two atomic bombs has added to the fears that already filled the souls of men and nations. One conference called to promote peace on earth adjourned with all sorts of problems unsolved. Another gathering seems to have intensified the direct forebodings. Unfortunately, neither meeting opened with prayer. A third has been convened, and doubtless others will follow. All the while prayerful fathers and mothers of teen-age boys keep shivering because of hypothetical

World War III. "Men and brethren, what shall we do"—to promote peace in our time?

When shall we as a people, with the others who fought against the Axis powers, fall down before God and confess our sins? After we have sought and found His pardon for our share in causing World War II, we can begin to plead for His blessing in the form of world-wide peace and brotherhood. All the while we should learn from President Harry S. Truman at the opening session of the peace parley in San Francisco: "If we do not want to die together in war, we must learn to live together in peace."

CHAPTER 12

THE IDEAL PASTOR FOR DAYS OF PEACE

I Samuel 12

EVERY PARISH MINISTER COULD STUDY SAMUEL'S FAREWELL ADDRESS with profit. So could the lay leaders of any congregation in quest of a pastor. The glowing words of the prophet set up ideals that go far to determine the character of a strong man's ministry in days of rebuilding. The three things that the prophet stressed long ago still bulk large in the life and work of every man called of God to become the leader of a parish church. With such a pastor any normal congregation will solve its problems and become a power in the work of the Kingdom. Without such a leader the home church will likely mark time, or even lose its influence for good. And yet in our days of reconstruction, many a fertile field lies untilled because no minister stands ready to serve as the parish leader. Whenever a strong man becomes a pastor, to what should he aspire?

1. *The ideal pastor is blameless in character* (vv. 1-5). The opening verses make clear what it means for a pastor to be a good man. As a practical observer our old friend Samuel has long since learned to think and speak concretely. Well does he know the pitfalls that lie in the pathway of a young clergyman. Doubtless the prophet is recalling the misdeeds of his own ministerial sons, as well as those of Eli's boys. Samuel himself has never yielded to the lure of money. He has not otherwise abused the powers given from above. He need not assure his friends that he has never stolen any man's wife, or dallied with any woman's affections. Like Dwight L. Moody, in a calling

that daily exposed him to such temptations, Samuel has kept himself unspotted from the world. For a minister that signifies freedom from greed, from ambition, and from lust.

A clergyman of this type excels as a pastor. Samuel does not allude to that aspect of his daily work. He takes for granted that the spiritual leader of God's children will show concern about their souls. Everywhere in these twelve chapters of First Samuel he has revealed his love for people. Because he has long since won their admiration, his influence has become unbounded. Of such a leader it could be said, as it often has been about Robert E. Lee: "That sort of man accomplishes more by lifting his little finger than many a would-be leader could do by shouting all day." Such a mighty influence flows out unconsciously.[1] As Oliver Goldsmith wrote about the village parson, he "allured to brighter worlds, and led the way."

First of all, the minister of God needs to be a good man. And yet a committee in search of a new pastor inquires first about almost everything else: "Is he a good talker and a good looker? A good mixer and a good dresser? A good executive and a jolly good fellow? Does he enjoy good health? Does he have a good wife?" All of these items belong in such a list. But why stress the by-products? First of all comes character, and that not of a grandmotherly darling. Stalwart character tempered with Christlike gentleness stands out in a worthy minister at any time, above all in the critical years that follow global strife. First he should be a man of God!

2. *He is gifted as a teacher* (vv. 6-18). The ideal pastor teaches all day, whenever he mingles with human beings. At present Samuel appears before us in the "pulpit." He cherishes the ideal of a teaching ministry, somewhat like that of Ezra, who "set his heart to seek the law of the Lord, and to do it, and to teach in

---

[1] See Horace Bushnell's famous sermon "Unconscious Influence," in *The New Life* (London, 1892), pp. 118-32.

Israel statutes and ordinances." [2] In the Hebrew this term "set his heart" means that he made it his chief aim in life. This verse in Ezra affords a miniature likeness of such a preacher as Samuel. Whenever he spoke he endeavored to do two things: to get every hearer right with God, and then to lead everyone in doing the will of the Most High. For an object lesson of his "pulpit work," take the heart of this Bible chapter. Even in such a brief summary you can find certain basic elements of a popular teaching ministry, a ministry for the common people.

The speaker uses facts, facts, facts. He employs all sorts of facts, but with two reservations. He chooses facts that bear on the subject in hand, facts that interest the people whom he addresses. For object lessons of factual preaching turn to the reported sayings of our Lord, especially His parables. Likewise consult the sermons of the Apostle Paul, as reported in the Book of the Acts. For a "homiletical commentary" on these addresses turn to a book by a professor at Columbia University and note how he uses the Apostle's sermons as models for young folk who are learning to write.[3]

More recent examples of factual preaching appear in the published sermons of Harry Emerson Fosdick and Ralph W. Sockman. Other object lessons, more directly biblical, abound in the sermons of James S. Stewart, of Edinburgh, and the late William M. Clow, of Glasgow. Perhaps unfortunately, this kind of pulpit work calls for wide knowledge and unusual skill. As for vast generalizations, devoid of facts, often they come without effort. Then they do little good. Obviously the Church needs here and there a statesman who can expound the basic philosophy of our religion. But as a rule such a pulpit style harks from the Middle Ages, not from the Bible. Search the Scriptures and see

[2] Ezra 7:10.
[3] Charles S. Baldwin, *The English Bible a Guide to Writing* (Macmillan, 1917), pp. 6-53, *et passim.*

whether the prophets and the apostles spoke to the common people concretely or abstractly. Then go and do likewise!

In the "sermon" by our aged friend the recital of facts leads up to his interpretation (vv. 13-15). Why bring out facts, however interesting, unless you make clear what they mean? Preaching calls for the interpretation of life today, in light that comes from God today. That must have been Samuel's ideal. In the light of God's dealings with the fathers, he called on the people to get right with the Lord. By way of strengthening the appeal he showed the folly of the opposite course. Time after time in the Old Testament, as well as in the New, "Yea, Yea" comes before "Nay, Nay." In our era of postwar uncertainty and dread both lights and shadows need to appear in the pulpit. But there ought to be vastly more of light than of shadow.

The last three verses in our Bible paragraph show how the preacher moves the will of the "friend in the pew." As here employed, the "will" means the entire personality in action. At least in popular preaching, every real sermon moves the will of the hearer. The man in the pulpit can reach and affect the will in only two ways: by appealing to the head or to the heart. Samuel used both ways, especially the latter. He stated facts clearly and strongly; that is good. He showed what they meant in the lives of his hearers; that is better. He guided the "layman" in doing the will of God as revealed in the sermon; that is best of all.

Once again, search the Scriptures. Then ask how well we present-day ministers are preaching. The ablest of our divines speak with absorbing human interest. But such pulpit masters as Charles H. Spurgeon and Thomas Chalmers made more of an impact on conscience and will. Why should we not keep the modern fashion of stressing human interest, and then use it as an instrument of divine power? [4] Fortunately, such dynamic preach-

[4] For more light here turn to Henry H. Farmer, *The Servant of the Word,* Scribner, 1942; and Charles H. Dodd, *The Apostolic Preaching and Its Developments,* Willett, Clark, 1937.

ing has never perished from the earth. Of late there has been a return to the ideals of Samuel. Listen to him now!

"Stand still and see this great thing, which the Lord will do before your eyes." Note the direct address. Now and again throughout the discourse the prophet speaks to his hearers. In each case he does it lovingly and without apology. As a father he pleads with God's children. Toward the end the prophet speaks as one with authority. "Thus saith the Lord!" The hour has come for God to declare Himself in action. He has been making ready for a visible demonstration of His power. At the time of the wheat harvest in the Holy Land He sent forth thunder. After the message from His servant, the Almighty sounded His "Amen."

George Whitefield once had something of the same experience while he was preaching. Afterward someone asked him for a copy of the sermon that had made such a tremendous impression. The evangelist replied that he would give the other a copy on one condition—he must supply the lightning and thunder that had driven home the message of the hour. Should every sermon leave such a mighty impression of power from on high? Nay, verily! As a rule the Lord speaks not "through the earthquake, wind, and fire" but through a "still, small voice of calm." Ofttimes what John Henry Jowett termed "the wooing note" proves to be God's way of reaching and moving the will.

Nevertheless, too much of our pulpit work lacks power. As a witness give heed to Woodrow Wilson, himself a son of the manse as well as a lover of the Church. When he served as President of Princeton University he always selected the minister to preach in the chapel on the Lord's Day. During that same period, on November 8, 1909, he spoke to the students at McCormick Seminary in Chicago. There he stressed the importance of appealing to the conscience and the will of the individual hearer:

THE IDEAL PASTOR FOR DAYS OF PEACE

I have heard a great deal of preaching, and I have heard most of it with respect. But I have heard a great deal of it with disappointment, because I felt that it had nothing to do with me. So many preachers whom I hear use the Gospel in order to expound some of the difficulties of modern thought. But only now and then does a minister direct upon me personally the raking fire of examination which consists in taking out of the Scriptures individual, concrete examples of men situated as I suppose myself to be situated, and searching me with the question—

How are you individually measuring up to the standard which in Holy Writ we know to have been exacted of this man and that? [5]

3. *He is mighty in prayer* (vv. 19-25). The prophet Samuel appears to have excelled as an intercessor. Was he not the son of a woman who prayed and the pupil of a man who interceded? Did not Samuel as a leader of men rely chiefly on prayer? [6] As the present chapter of First Samuel makes clear, he had long since formed the habit of interceding for the people. Doubtless he had also taught the most spiritual-minded of them to pray. Why should it not be so today in every parish? Are not many of our people now as fearful of the future as those who asked for the intercessions of Samuel?

In the hour of dread concern about the unknown morrow the eyes of those deluded mortals were opened. At last they could see wherein they had sinned. Hitherto they may not have understood why their asking for a king had made Samuel grieve. Sometimes it takes a storm to clear the air. If so, all of us on earth have had abundant opportunities of late to see that we are sinners in the eyes of our holy God. Who then will pray for us?

Herein lies a searching test of a pastor's work. How often do his people ask him to intercede for them, as a family of God's children? How many of them seek him out, one at a time, to tell

---

[5] *College and State* (Harper, 1925), II, 178-79.
[6] Cf. I Sam. 7:5-6 and 15:11.

of sin and to ask for prayer? When people make such a request, do they hear the minister reply with the prophet of old: "Far be it from me that I should sin against the Lord in ceasing to pray for you"? That word "ceasing" points back over years of intercession for God's wandering sheep. What else does it mean to be a pastor? How can the minister neglect to pray for people without sinning against God?

Does anyone long to become a worthy pastor? Who of us does not? The secret lies largely in learning to pray. If the minister intercedes for the people, and then leads them in doing the will of God, he will grow more and more like Samuel. Blameless in character, gifted in teaching, mighty in prayer! What an ideal, especially for our days of disillusionment after a deadly war. In every parish may such a leader as Samuel become the key man in the work of the Kingdom!

Part Two

THE RULER WHO FAILS IN REBUILDING

FIRST SAMUEL, CHAPTERS 13-31

CHAPTER 13

THE FOLLIES OF AN IMPETUOUS KING

I Samuel 13

FROM THIS POINT ON WE SHALL WITNESS THE BREAKING DOWN OF A strong personality. At present we are to consider the first of the major blunders committed by King Saul. We shall not think of them as sins, for we have reason to surmise that he gradually became the victim of intermittent mental disorders. While we note that the Scriptures disapprove of his impetuous actions, we find that in the long run they deal with him gently. If we assume that often he was beside himself, we can see how a person once blessed of God may become a stumbling block, if not a menace.

King Saul appears to have represented what William James styled "the impulsive temperament." Over against persons of this type stand those whom he termed the "reflective." Sometimes we assume that impetuous persons must be weaker and worse than reflective ones. Do we forget that Jacob and David, as well as Peter and Luther, with countless others blessed of God, belonged to the impulsive type? Doubtless the ideal man, like our Lord, would combine the two temperaments in a sort of stable equilibrium. However, most of us incline one way or the other. No one can alter his basic disposition. But everyone can make the most of his God-given powers as well as his human limitations. All of that Saul failed to do. Hence he made shipwreck of a promising career.

1. *The menace of an invading host* (vv. 1-7). The first two Bible paragraphs bring out the need of a commander with poise and self-control. The Philistines had invaded the land and met

with a temporary setback. Then they had swooped down with what seemed irresistible might. They threatened to overrun the country and to enslave the people. The destined field of battle lay at Michmash, in the hill country a few miles north and east of Jerusalem. As the men of Israel went out to battle under the leadership of King Saul, their hearts were all a-tremble. In an hour of crisis such "warriors" may do more harm than good. Outnumbered by forces far better armed, how could those trembling Hebrews expect to triumph? Their only hope lay in God. Under Him, they should have been able to rely on their king. Unfortunately, they found Saul impetuous and unpredictable. Such a leader, alas, may do more harm than good.

2. *The folly of acting rashly* (vv. 8-15a). The king felt that he ought to tarry at Gilgal, and there do nothing for seven days, until Samuel came to offer sacrifices.[1] A man of Saul's temperament would rather do anything else than wait. An athlete of this type keeps playing offside, thus bringing penalties on the whole team. Above all does the believer in God need to wait quietly upon the Lord. In His loving providence the hour will come for action. Then the leader and his forces must strike. For a series of object lessons, both in "watchful waiting" and in aggressive action, turn to the records of George Washington in the Revolutionary War. Then thank God for his self-control.

At the end of the appointed time, the prophet had not appeared. Hence the king took matters into his own hands. Without any warrant he offered up sacrifices to God. Even if he could have done so under a divine commission, his seven days of chafing would have left him in no mood for leading others in worship. But when has an impetuous person ever paused to consider the wisdom or the timeliness of his impulsive deeds? Something must be done, and that right now. The man appointed of God has failed to appear. Why not step into the breach? Who can

[1] See I Sam. 10:8.

tell how many of earth's tragedies have been caused by such rashness?

A leader of this type can always plead an excuse. In fact, he may have more than one. King Saul blamed Samuel for not appearing on scheduled time. Then, too, he saw that the people had begun to scatter. Hence, as he said, he "forced" himself to act. Like the men whom he should have commanded, he must have been gripped by fear. In the presence of invading hosts, ready to swoop down upon the shivering people, why should not their king render sacrifices to God? Who but He could deliver? Thus the impetuous ruler brought down on his head the judgment of the Almighty.

According to Phillips Brooks, the offering of those sacrifices involved "the unwarrantable performance of a religious rite." "Thou hast done foolishly; thou hast not kept the commandment of the Lord thy God." These words of the prophet may seem needlessly severe. But remember that King Saul was on trial. During those days of watchful waiting he missed the opportunity to show self-restraint, calmly waiting until the hour called for action. He likewise failed to prove that he could keep to his own appointed tasks and not infringe on the province of another man appointed of God. Is it asking too much that a ruler think first about God and then about others? Must his own self always come first?

The rebuke from God's spokesman dealt with deliberate disobedience. Of his own free will the king had done what he felt to be against the counsels of his God. Hence he had forfeited his right to serve as the ruler of God's people. That place of honor would soon be handed over to a younger man of the Lord's own choosing. Because of such judgment from above, Saul's heart must have quailed. From this time on he appears to have become a different kind of person. Hence his followers must have kept asking each other: "What has come over our king? He used to be as brave as a lion and as gentle as a lamb. Now he appears to be full of fears and to have lost his poise. Would that he might regain his oldtime charm!"

3. *The lack of national preparedness* (vv. 19-23). Our present Bible chapter does not tell us the outcome of the warfare. In lieu of that, the account shows one reason for the fears of King Saul and his followers. These closing verses remind us that we are looking back on rough and primitive days. The record also brings out the lack of constructive leadership on the part of King Saul. In both farming and fighting his people had become dependent on their foes. If David had been in control, he would have encouraged them to become self-reliant, and he would have shown them how to "live at home." Wholly apart from issues of safety and self-defense, he would have known that farmers ought to be largely self-supporting.

What do such backward people need? Under God, they must have the right sort of leadership. During the time of the Judges, when strong champions emerged only once in a while, the Israelites had slipped back into barbarism. They could not even sharpen their hoes, not to speak of their spears. In the face of invading hosts why should such childish folk not feel helpless and hopeless? When they looked up to their king what did they see? A mighty statesman with a constructive program for the upbuilding of his fatherland? No! They found Saul with no plan for developing the nation and with no power to control himself. Reluctantly they concluded that he had been weighed in God's balances and there found wanting. Do laymen ever have cause to feel so about their pastor?

CHAPTER 14

THE CRUELTY OF RECKLESS VOWS

I Samuel 14

HERE WE FIND ANOTHER OF THE CONTRASTS IN WHICH OUR BOOK abounds. Over against Saul the king we behold Jonathan his son. Thus far we have been thinking about Saul as fairly young, but now we must look on him as a man of middle age. Perhaps we have been overstressing his youth. Here we first become acquainted with the son. Whenever he stands forth in the Bible, Jonathan leaves a wholesome impression. How could such a well-poised, God-fearing young man spring from such a rash, God-defying father?

Whatever the explanation, the facts about the younger man afford a foil to bring out sharply the rashness and the lack of religion in the king. For the present, though, the son must give way to the father. In King Saul we have the materials for a case study in the practical workings of rashness. The discussion which follows makes little reference to the right sort of vows. In marriage, and elsewhere in life, a good man pledges his honor that he will hold true unto death. What sort of vows does a rash king utter? Let us see, first by contrast.

1. *The practical meaning of faith* (vv. 1-23). The first half of our chapter shows how faith works in the life of a godly warrior. The record makes clear how a soldier can be bold and resourceful instead of lacking in self-control. Accompanied only by an armor-bearer, young Jonathan steals into the midst of the slumbering Philistines. There by courage and resourcefulness he causes a panic and a rout. If anyone ever asks him to explain what he has

done, modestly he will reply that he has simply trusted in God.

The words of the young warrior to his armor-bearer show the practical meaning of faith: "It may be that the Lord will work for us; for there is no restraint to the Lord to save by many or by few." The stress here falls on God's arithmetic. Another case, somewhat parallel, appears in Judges 7:2-22. There young Gideon, battling against overwhelming odds, reduced his ranks from thirty-two thousand to three hundred. With that little band he "put to flight the armies of the aliens." Any one of those three hundred troopers might have posed for a statue of "God's Unknown Soldier." The spirit of Jonathan's armor-bearer shows how the right sort of leader evokes loyalty in his followers: "Do all that is in thy heart: turn thee, behold, I am with thee according to thy heart." Could Jonathan or Gideon ever have done the will of the Lord without such followers?

What then do we understand by faith? How does it differ from bravado? Practically, faith means human weakness laying hold of divine strength in order to accomplish "the impossible." Young Jonathan trusted in God. For that reason he depended on his armor-bearer. If there had been three hundred followers, or three hundred thousand, the leader would have relied upon them to do the will of God. Strange as it may sound at first, the young leader also believed in himself. This, too, enters largely into the practical meaning of faith. Trust the Lord supremely; depend on others largely; rely on self humbly. God first. Others second. Self last. What a philosophy for a life of service!

2. *The cruelty of reckless vows* (vv. 24-46). In contrast to the brightness of young Jonathan's faith the artist shows the blackness of King Saul's folly. At the very time when the young man was putting the enemy to confusion and flight, the impetuous father was uttering a needless vow which might have caused the death of his beloved son: "Cursed be the man that eateth any food until it be evening, and I be avenged on mine enemies."

What incredible stupidity! When men are fighting with all their might, they need food as much as harvest hands. Fasting may have its place, but not on the field of battle. Not only was the vow nonsensical; it was wrong, diabolically wrong. If it had been carried out it would have involved the death of every warrior who took a morsel of food that day. Young Jonathan ate wild honey, and he was condemned to die.

We think of youth as headstrong and irrepressible. We forget that "there's no fool like an old fool." Here the father showed the cruelty of reckless vows. When he spoke those fateful words he committed a sin. If he had been able to execute his orders, he would have murdered his son, the crown prince. To take such an oath involves a deadly wrong; to carry it out is doubly damnable. Fortunately, the people intervened to prevent King Saul from slaying his son. Even so, the facts afford materials for a case study. Why is it wrong to utter such a vow, and doubly wrong to carry it out? Here we face a question both difficult and delicate.

Why did the king utter those fateful words? Doubtless because he did not stop to think. Why did he later attempt to execute that decree of death, even though it involved his beloved son? Perhaps because of the pride that makes a strong man afraid to take a dare, and doubly afraid to back down when he has done the initial wrong. When Saul found that he had committed the first egregious blunder, he should have made an about-face. To be guilty of a second wrong, far more tragic, can never rectify a false start. When a strong leader discovers that he has played the fool, publicly, he tells his men that he has erred. Then he cancels the orders. Why should any mortal try to pose as infallible? Why should a king have to be restrained by his people? "Shall Jonathan die, who hath wrought this great salvation in Israel?"

How did those indignities affect the son's attitude toward his father? Apparently not at all, at least not adversely. Jonathan may have known that his father's heart normally overflowed with kindness and that some evil spirit had begun to make him cruel. Whatever the feelings of the crown prince, he forgave those deadly wrongs. Never afterward did he display bitterness toward his headstrong father. Like Joseph in the latter part of Genesis, Jonathan seems to have loved God so much that he took delight in rendering good for evil. This may be why the crown prince often makes us think about the Lord Jesus Christ.

3. *The other cases in the Scriptures* (vv. 47-52). The discussion here concerns only such "oaths" as involve cruelty to the innocent. Other examples appear in the Bible. Rather than back down after he had uttered a foolish vow, Jephthah seems to have offered up his daughter as a living sacrifice.[1] Even if he "merely" condemned her to a state of perpetual virginity, as some scholars suppose, would not a Hebrew maiden rather have died? Later in Old Testament times King Darius cast Daniel into the lions' den because of a bootless "pledge of honor."[2] In New Testament days King Herod carried out a silly promise made to a shameless girl, even though by doing so he caused the death of a mighty prophet.[3] Afterward certain Jewish bigots thirsted after the blood of the Apostle Paul. They vowed that they would not eat or drink until they had hounded him to death.[4] They must have endured a protracted fast, for they never again laid eyes on that servant of God. "Surely the wrath of man shall praise thee."[5]

A glance back over these five cases brings to light a disconcerting truth. In every instance the culprit, or the culprits, had passed beyond the days of youth. Every one of those respon-

[1] Judg. 11:29-40.
[2] Dan. 6:1-27.
[3] Matt. 14:1-12.
[4] Acts 23:21.
[5] Psa. 76:10; cf. Rom. 8:28.

sible for a bootless "pledge of honor" seems to have been a man of middle age, or even older. And yet we ministers of middle years and beyond often pride ourselves on our poise. We sometimes prate about the irresponsibility of young people. Why do we not face the facts? No one age group can claim any monopoly, either in the way of virtue or in the way of vice. Like every other form of moral evil, lack of self-control tends to increase with the years, unless restrained by grace.

As for the taking of needless vows, a careful study of these cases will lead to a definite conclusion: such a course is not only unwise but also wrong. No one but a person devoid of wisdom and honor would be guilty of such sin. Only a coward would deliberately refuse to change his stand when he discovered that he had played the fool with his lips. Often the wrong lies in the motive even more than in the deed itself: "Be not rash with thy mouth, and let not thy heart be hasty to utter anything before God." [6] In view of such lofty ideals about human speech, who of us can refrain from confessing his sins of rashness?

What are your home church and its minister doing to inculcate these ideals found in Holy Writ? Are you rearing boys like Jonathan? If so, you are helping to avert such tragedies as darkened the closing days of King Saul. In order to rear young men like Jonathan, the local church and her pastor must learn how to inculcate duty as well as doctrine. "The Scriptures principally teach what man is to believe concerning God, and what duty God requires of man."

---

[6] Eccles. 5:2.

111

CHAPTER 15

THE WORKINGS OF A MAN'S CONSCIENCE

I Samuel 15

THIS CHAPTER OF FIRST SAMUEL AFFORDS MATERIAL FOR A STUDY IN the workings of a man's conscience. As for the meaning of "conscience," no savant has ever framed a satisfactory definition. The following may serve as a description: Conscience is the God-given power that shows a man the right from the wrong; impels him to do the right, not the wrong; approves him when he does the right, and rebukes him when he does the wrong. At least that is how conscience ought to work. In a man's life, as with his watch, there needs to be a perfect standard outside the man's self. Apart from the Lord Jesus, no man's conscience has ever operated ideally.

The experience of King Saul brings to light some of the ways in which conscience fails. Even so, a man ought to obey this inner voice, much as he should rely on his watch. If either of them gets out of order, so that it reports the facts incorrectly, or not at all, he should go at once to an expert. When the conscience of King Saul required careful adjustment, he found in Samuel an expert much like our Lord, who "knew what was in man." [1] Every community today needs such a counselor, to whom anyone may turn for help when his conscience fails to work.

1. *The testing of a man's conscience* (vv. 1-3). These opening verses relate to the extermination of the Amalekites. The record ascribes to the Almighty this command: "Spare them not; but

---

[1] John 2:25b.

112

slay both man and woman, infant and suckling, ox and sheep, camel and ass." These sweeping injunctions raise a serious question, one that the present writer cannot begin to answer. Of course he knows that we are looking back on primitive days,[2] long before men and nations began to know the Golden Rule. As with Benito Mussolini, we feel that Agag deserved to die. Whatever our attitude toward these ethical issues, we should recognize one fact: King Saul felt sure that he should have exterminated those foes. When he failed to do so, he felt equally sure that he had disobeyed God.

A case somewhat parallel appears in a recent novel, one of the worthier best sellers. In *How Green Was My Valley,* by Richard Llewellyn,[3] the action centers in a valley of Wales. There the simplehearted mining folk have never felt the need of law courts and policemen. One day a brute in man's clothing violates the person of a little girl and then leaves her dead. As vigilantes, the men of the community take the law into their own hands. First they make sure of the culprit's guilt, concerning which there can be no question. After a "trial" in public, the girl's menfolk bear him away into the mountains, from which he never returns. Afterward the executioners never allude to his fate.

Who will dare to say that those men did wrong? How could they have dealt with that offense more justly? Similar drastic action proved needful on the West Coast during early days. Bands of self-appointed vigilantes meted out justice swiftly, at times without mercy. On the other hand, we all deplore the mob spirit that leads to lynching. With equal dismay we learn about ruthless deeds on many a battlefield. When shall we mortals learn to distinguish between right and wrong?

Now let us face our question directly. It concerns the com-

[2] See Marcus Dods, *Israel's Iron Age,* pp. 7-10; also the apocryphal Book of Wisdom, 12:3-27.
[3] Macmillan, 1940, pp. 202-8.

promise between what a man feels to be his duty and what he actually does. Even if Saul could have conjured up an excuse for sparing Agag, how could he have justified his keeping the booty? By doing so he yielded to the sort of greed that has marked almost every conqueror in history. In view of such black facts, what will the prophet say? What will he do? Rest assured that he will serve as the incarnate conscience of people rightly called children. Why does the prophet speak, if not to show the right from the wrong, to urge the doing of the right, to approve it when done, and to rebuke the wrong?

2. *The awakening of a man's conscience* (vv. 10-16). Before he approached the king, Samuel needed to know how the matter stood in the eyes of God. He still loved the impetuous king and felt loath to cause him pain. Reluctantly Samuel learned that the man whom he had anointed as ruler over Israel had been rejected by the Lord. Not even the wisest and best of ministers can hope to become an infallible interpreter of God's holy will. When the prophet learned that God had "repented" concerning the selection of Saul as king, he wondered what that could mean. Surely the Lord had never done wrong; how then could He seem sorry? Evidently the word "repented" indicated a change of attitude. As often elsewhere,[4] the Bible here speaks of God as though He were a man. Such anthropomorphism need not lead anyone astray.

Before he dared to address the king, Samuel spent a night in prayer, pouring out his soul unto God. Like Jacob of old, who wrestled with the angel until the coming of the dawn, the prophet needed grace to accept the will of God. Before the morning broke he submitted to the wisdom that cometh down from above. In that new spirit of compliance with the will of God,

[4] E.g., Gen. 3:8; 8:21; 11:5, 7; II Sam. 24:16; Jer. 18:8-10; Jonah 3:10, *et al.* See Samuel R. Driver, *An Introduction to the Literature of the Old Testament* (Scribner, 1902), pp. 9, 121.

the prophet went forth to meet the disobedient king. Somewhat like Samuel, Queen Victoria is said to have thought overnight and prayed before she arrived at any important decision. Then she could act with assurance and a sense of finality. Note the contrast between such self-control—or rather, God-control—and the rashness of King Saul. Why did he often leap into action before he looked up to God?

When the prophet speaks to the king, what does the guilty one reply? The words of Saul to his former adviser show the evasions of a conscience out of order. In such a case there need be no resort to a lie detector. Listen to the boast of the king: "I have performed the commandment of the Lord!" Then speaks the prophet: "What meaneth this bleating of the sheep in mine ears, and the lowing of the oxen which I hear?" The man with a painful conscience has a reply on the tip of his tongue: "The people spared the best of the sheep and of the oxen, to sacrifice unto the Lord thy God." What a way to appease a prophet! Saul was supposed to be the leader of those people. How could he blame them for his wrongdoing? Is not this our old human nature? Blame everybody in sight—except yourself!

3. *The probing of a man's conscience* (vv. 17-23). Now we are to watch a master surgeon at work on a quivering soul. Note how he strikes down to the source of the trouble. When a man of God must deal with a king who has disobeyed his conscience and then refused to confess his fault, the time has passed for gentle measures. Boldly the seer makes three charges, no one of which his hearer can deny. Taken together, they show how a strong man gives way when he has unlimited power over his fellow men. The modest, unassuming Saul has changed, and that for the worse!

First comes the charge of ingratitude to God. To that Lord who has done everything good for the king, Saul has shown naught but thanklessness. This ought to concern us all, for

115

ingratitude to God has been styled "America's favorite sin." Then follows the charge of disobedience to the Most High. Last of all comes the accusation of irresponsibility. Instead of accepting the onus of his misdeeds, the king has tried to shift the blame to his unsuspecting people. What a threefold indictment! Because of these misdeeds, and the inner weakness that they reveal, this man henceforth shall be counted unworthy of God's favor and of the kingship.

Out of this sorry mess has come one of the most memorable sayings ever uttered before the days of our Lord: "To obey is better than sacrifice, and to hearken than the fat of rams." In other words, righteousness stands out above worship. Like the other prophets, Samuel believed in the public worship of God. The Hebrew seers knew that the best of their ways in worship had come from Him. Still they insisted that no religious ceremonies, however correct in themselves, could serve as substitutes for righteousness. They declared that true religion consisted in right attitudes toward God and men. To engage in public worship without having hearts right with God constituted superstition, if not magic. Is there not a need for such a message today?

4. *The outcry of a man's conscience* (vv. 24-31). What response will come from the king? First he voices an abject confession of sin. His words impress us as simple, direct, and manly: "I have sinned!" Here the king displays none of his former evasiveness. In substance, he says, without one plea, "I did it all myself. I alone am at fault. I have sinned." He does not even take refuge in plural pronouns. As for his motive, that seems to have been fear of the people. "What will they think?" Why should a king ever cater to the childish opinions of the people over whom he ought to rule? Did he sincerely repent? Was he truly penitent because of his sins against God, or was he merely rueful because

of the consequences to himself? Sincere contrition springs from grief at heart because of failure to do God's holy will.

After the confession of sin there ensues the king's plea for mercy. Strange to tell, he does not ask the prophet to intercede with God, but to grant pardon himself. Here again, the suppliant's religion, so called, seems to have taken the form of magic. He appears to have lost all personal touch with God. Twice in this chapter the king speaks to Samuel about "thy God." The man whose religion comes by proxy finds in it no refuge from the storms of life. If Saul had paused to think, he would have known that God alone could pardon his sin and give him peace of mind. He was waiting to do so through Samuel as a personal counselor, but not for a man whose religion was secondhand.

In response to the king's frenzied appeal for mercy the seer pronounced on him words of judgment. At first the doom here described seems needlessly severe. But remember that this king stood out as the public representative of the holy God. Even if his penitence had been sincere and deep-seated, he would have lacked the sort of resolution that marks "a man born to be king." "Thou hast rejected the word of the Lord, and the Lord hath rejected thee from being king over Israel." As a symbol of what the king would soon have to suffer, when Saul laid hold of the prophet's robe it rent asunder. Instead of reaching out by faith to touch the mantle of the Living God, the weakening monarch clutched the garment of the Lord's servant. There stood the king, holding in his hand a piece of torn raiment. What a symbol of human weakness, without God and without hope! [5]

5. *The seal on a man's conscience* (vv. 32-35). These closing verses bring out two scenes that the king was never to forget. First he stood by to watch the aged prophet hewing Agag in pieces. Much as we wish that Samuel himself had not slain the

---

[5] For a striking contrast see Luke 8:43-48; also Lloyd C. Douglas, *The Robe*, Houghton, Mifflin, 1942.

old-time Hitler, still we acknowledge that the alien leader deserved to die. Can we likewise put ourselves in the place of
King Saul? How must he have felt? He might have sat for a
study by that master in word painting who wrote about the
conscience as "seared with a hot iron." [6]

Still another dismal recollection would haunt the soul of the
king until his dying day. Once and forever he had bidden
farewell to aged Samuel, who had departed in sorrow, not in
anger. Never again would the vacillating king look upon the
face of the friend who had stood for him in the place of God.
Never more would Saul hear the voice that had pleaded for
obedience to the will of the Lord. When the two men parted in
silence and tears, each of them knew that the separation had come
because one of them had turned his back upon God. Can you
wonder that the bewildered king began to feel God-forsaken?

If there were need of a moral it might refer to the parish
minister. If he wishes to deal with strong men, one after another,
he must possess courage born of faith. How else could the pastor
bring such a man as Saul face to face with his sins? How could
Samuel as the ministering servant of God speak the truth about
the man who had led the people astray? Apart from divine grace,
how can any of us serve as the pastoral counselor of such a rash
and impetuous mortal as King Saul?

As for the disease in this man's soul, the facts appear in a
moving sermon by Cardinal Newman, under the heading "Will-
fulness, the Sin of Saul." The following has been slightly
amended:

The spirit of Saul still lives, . . . the principle of cleaving and
breaking down all divine ordinances, instead of building up. And
with Saul's sin, Saul's portion awaits his followers,—distraction,
aberration; the hiding of God's countenance; imbecility, rashness,

[6] See I Tim. 4:2.

118

and changeableness in their counsels; judicial blindness; fear of the multitude; alienation from good men and faithful friends; subserviency to their worst foes, the kings of Amalek and the wizards of Endor. . . . Such is ever the righteous doom of those who trust their own wills more than God's Word.[7]

[7] See *Fifteen Sermons Preached Before the University of Oxford* (London, 1872), p. 172.

CHAPTER 16

THE CHOICE OF A NATIONAL LEADER

I Samuel 16

THE MOST IMPORTANT EVENT IN THE LIFE OF A NATION MAY BE the selection of a new leader. If the outgoing ruler has proved unworthy, or if he has tarried in office too long, the choice of his successor becomes a matter of tremendous concern. Above all, this issue looms large during the years that follow a war. For living examples, look across the seven seas.

If anyone asks what all of this has to do with religion, let the answer come from President John A. Mackay, of Princeton Seminary: "It is not the business of the Church to create a new social order, but to create the creators of that new social order." In State as in Church, under God, almost everything good depends on the right sort of leadership. Not only must the Church rear sons worthy to rule. She must also guide her members in helping to elect the men of God's own choosing. In short, He gives us as good leaders as we deserve. Often He does far better!

1. *Approach the choice in the spirit of worship* (vv. 1-5). For a concrete example of the right method in choosing a leader turn to the scene at the home of Jesse, a sheepman at Bethlehem. There the prophet Samuel follows the guidance of the Lord. That inner leading comes while he is busy with others who seek to learn the will of God. In a way the scene reminds us of family worship back in a dear farm home. Seven stalwart sons join with their father in doing homage to God, their Invisible King. What a picture of the possibilities that lie unrevealed in a household blessed with worthy sons!

2. *Choose the man after God's own heart* (vv. 6-13). Once again the record brings to view a striking contrast. Over against the theoretical judgments of the prophet stands the practical wisdom of Almighty God. Who but He can know the hearts of His servants now assembled for worship? But He does not rigidly enforce his will. Hence the tension mounts while we ask: Who is to have the right of way, God or man? In all such matters we human beings cherish opinions of our own. It never occurs to Samuel that God may pass by all of these seven sons. Why does he blithely assume that the Lord will agree with him?

Give heed to a word from the throne! "Man looketh on the outward appearance." If this were all that a king required, who could make a better showing than King Saul? Physically, he seemed to possess all the marks of a man born to rule. Nevertheless, he failed. And yet Samuel, if left to himself, would have chosen another person of the same type. With feelings of inner satisfaction the prophet surveyed the oldest son of Jesse. Then in turn the man of God looked at the second, the third, and on to the last of the seven. As for the eighth, the youngest of the brood, no one dreamed that he might be the man chosen of God to serve as king. "My thoughts are not your thoughts, neither are your ways my ways, saith the Lord." [1]

"The Lord looketh on the heart." He knew that young David had in his soul the root of the matter. As with Joseph when a lad, the choice of the Lord fell on the stripling who had already learned to be loyal. No doubt young David was handsome. His physical prowess equaled that of his brothers. But, better by far, he had formed the habit of doing the will of God. So the young man stood ready for service far more exacting than that of tending sheep. As long as he kept close to his God, David would rightly be known as the Shepherd King. Can it be acci-

---

[1] Isa. 55:8.

dental that in Hebrew history such leaders as Joseph, Moses, and David served their apprenticeship as keepers of the flock? To this very hour do we not think of the local minister as the "pastor"?

After the prophet had discovered the young man of God's choice, there came the ceremony of anointing. That use of consecrated oil symbolized the setting apart of the young man for the public service of God. Far more vital than anything that men could see, the sacred rite betokened an infilling by the Holy Spirit. Practically, the Holy Spirit means the power of God in the life of a man for service. Up to that hour of anointing, young David may have seemed a lad of promise, and nothing more. From that day on he could wield a power vastly higher than his own. Would that it were so with every man set apart to lead a nation in times of rebuilding after war!

3. *The Spirit of God departs from an unworthy leader* (vv. 14-23). In as far as human eyes could see, the first king of Israel had entered on his lifework with a promise superior to that of young David. On the purely human level, Saul possessed everything that heart could desire in a king. But in the course of time he began to depend on himself, not on God. More and more the ruler ceased to follow the counsels of Samuel. Whatever the explanation in terms of theology, the king gradually lost his sense of God's presence, as well as the assurance of His power. Hence the so-called ruler began to feel God-forsaken. "The Spirit of the Lord departed from Saul, and an evil spirit from the Lord troubled him."

These few words have been troubling readers of the Bible ever since the words were written. "An evil spirit from the Lord!" What does that mean? Who can tell? Evidently Saul no longer enjoyed the guidance and the blessing of the Lord. In the course of time his soul became the abode of a demonic spirit. In terms of our day he appears to have become "psychoneurotic." [2] Unlike most of us, the Hebrews ascribed to God almost everything human, whether good or bad. Hence they spoke of a malign influence as "an evil spirit from the Lord." Modern writers would report that Saul had become subject to intermittent mental aberrations. Whatever the terminology, it covers a multitude of hypothetical suppositions. The whole matter lies mainly in the realm of the unconscious, and that can be known only by the Almighty.

Somehow we should relate such things to the providence of God. Surely we believe that they occur with His permission. Sometimes, however, we forget that He allows what He may not approve. "Permission without sanction!" In our own time, He must have suffered a demonic spirit to enter the heart of Adolf Hitler. But no one would think of ascribing to God all the havoc wrought by the author of *Mein Kampf*. On a scale far smaller, and less tragic, the Lord seems to have let King Saul reap what he had sowed. In such a case is it unkind to say that both in body and in spirit most of our ills are self-imposed? According to Frederick W. Robertson, "in things spiritual, too, whatsoever a man soweth, that shall he also reap. Not something else, but *that!*" [3]

Another master preacher has dealt with our subject more directly. Under the heading "An Evil Spirit from the Lord," Phillips Brooks discusses this proposition:

A beneficent power, if we obey it, blesses and helps us; but the same power, if we disobey it, curses and ruins us. . . . Saul is obedient, and God is brightness, courage, hope, happiness. Saul disobeys, and his soul becomes melancholy, gloomy, irritable, sus-

[2] For a nontechnical discussion of such "casualties" in war, see George K. Pratt (psychiatric examiner, U. S. Armed Forces), *Soldier to Civilian, Problems of Readjustment,* Whittlesey House, 1944.

[3] See his well-known discourse "The Principle of the Spiritual Harvest," in *Sermons* (Harper, n.d.), pp. 158-68.

picious, envious, distracted. . . . There is no privilege which you cannot turn into a curse. God does love you, and will never cease to love you, no matter what you are, no matter where you go; . . . but His love shall be to you either a spirit of help or a spirit of harm, according to your obedience or disobedience to Him.[4]

Homiletically, this sermon reveals much about the way to use the Old Testament in the modern pulpit. The Boston preacher's emphasis falls on the positive contribution to our human needs, not on the difficulty of reconciling the biblical account with our "scientific" ways of thought. From this viewpoint look at the closing words of the message from the most beloved pastor of his day. Notice how he addresses the hearer kindly, and how the appeal comes home to the heart. Note too how an optimist can preach the gospel from such a part of the Old Testament:

This is the truth to preach to men and women who are in the midst of the reality and the solemnity of life. It is strong, manly doctrine. The Bible rings with it. All powerful and vital Christianity is full of it. It is not hard and cruel. It is not weak and sentimental. I beg you to take this truth. Let it fill your life. Let it make you serious, brave, thoughtful, hopeful and fearful both. Let it make you men of God, living in His service, rejoicing in His love, and feeling already in your obedient souls the power of His everlasting life.[5]

Our present Bible chapter is of interest to the pastoral counselor. From his practical point of view it shows the power of music to relieve the distress within a man's soul. In King Saul's lucid periods he sensed that he was no longer himself. He asked the attendants to secure a man skillful in playing the harp. When-

---

[4] *Sermons* (Dutton, 1910), IV, 297-316.

[5] *Ibid.*, p. 314.

ever a seizure appeared to be coming on, the music would still the tumult within his soul. In the long run, however, this way of dealing with the malady proved to be futile. When a strong man's mind becomes "jangled, out of tune and harsh," the causes lie beyond the reach of music.

The custom of employing music to allay storms within the soul appears elsewhere in literature. For instance, the practice must have been common in the time of Shakespeare. In *King Lear* Cordelia summons a physician to treat her afflicted father. The master of the healing art arranges that the unconscious king shall return to a state of awareness amid strains of soothing music. In comparatively recent times the novelist Turgenev suffered after the fashion of King Saul. The Russian writer discovered that "music helped him more than medicine." Indeed,

> Music hath charms to soothe the savage breast,
> To soften rocks, or bend a knotted oak.

The use of David's harp to drive away the evil spirit led Robert Browning to compose one of his most obscure poems. In fact, more than one bewildered reader has felt like applauding the king for hurling his javelin at the singer! However, the poem really does make sense. It shows how a lover of wide, open spaces can sing about flocks beside still waters, and then about joy in harvest fields. Gradually the melody leads up to the highest and holiest of human experiences on earth. At last the harpist beholds the glory of the coming Redeemer. Seldom has our most Christian poet drawn so close to the heart of all that we hold dear:

He who did most, shall bear most; the strongest shall stand the
    most weak.
'Tis the weakness in strength, that I cry for! my flesh, that I seek
In the Godhead! I seek and I find it. O Saul, it shall be

A Face like my face that receives thee; a Man like to me,
Thou shalt love and be loved by, forever: a Hand like this hand
Shall throw open the gates of new life to thee! See the Christ stand!

What if we cannot follow all the windings of thought and feeling within this mystical song? What if we cannot fathom all the depths suggested by the phrase "an evil spirit from the Lord"? At least we can discover one fact of increasing concern during times of rebuilding after a global war. Even in days of peace every community includes more than a few men and women with nervous disorders. After every war the number of these victims increases beyond computation. In any one case, whatever the medical diagnosis and treatment, the victim needs friendship, both human and divine.[6]

Where can the distraught soul find solace if not in the home church and in its pastor? Whenever the nervous wreck comes to the sanctuary or to the study, is he sure to receive the peace of God which passeth all understanding, as well as the joy that this old world cannot give or take away?

> Canst thou not minister to a mind diseased,
> Pluck from the memory a rooted sorrow,
> Raze out the written troubles of the brain,
> And with some sweet oblivious antidote
> Cleanse the stuffed bosom of that perilous stuff
> Which weighs upon the heart? [7]

In a high sense only the Lord Jesus can begin to work that healing within the soul. Today His love goes forth to everyone whose heart is filled with unrest and fear. He is waiting to drive out the evil spirit and to make the afflicted one whole. The heal-

---

[6] For a nontechnical discussion, not religious, see Carl Binger, *The Doctor's Job*, Norton, 1945.

[7] *Macbeth*, V, iii, 42-47.

ing touch of His dear hand is able to reach and cure the spirit as well as the body.

So let every home church and its pastor awake to the high privilege of forestalling these disorders within the soul. Most of them start in childhood. Let there be not only tender concern for every friend who has "lost the kindly light of reason." Let there also be loving care for every little boy who might otherwise go the way of King Saul.

CHAPTER 17

THE HEROISM OF GOD'S CHAMPION

I Samuel 17

WE COME NOW TO ONE OF THE MOST DRAMATIC SCENES IN THE
Old Testament. Only one other may excel this passage in dramatic power. That is the eighteenth chapter of First Kings.
There the prophet Elijah singlehanded prevails over the hosts of
Baal. Here young David triumphs over a mighty giant. This foe
appears to be all-powerful. With both Elijah and David the
contest goes on until the death of the enemy. In each case the
champion of the Lord's people stands out against the forces of
antigod. In such dramatic action the suspense grows out of a
conflict between two opposing powers, the one good and the
other evil. Here, then, behold a hero and a villain as they engage
in mortal combat for tremendous stakes.

What has all of this to do with religion? According to the
customary way of recounting the facts, nothing at all! Even in
Bible school on the Lord's Day a zealous teacher can present the
narrative as though it dealt with a prize fight between a Tunney
and a Dempsey. The passage itself, however, proceeds on a
higher level; or rather, the narrative moves on two different
planes. Thus the chapter embodies a striking contrast. In the first
half of the lengthy description the name of God emerges only
once, and that near the end. In the remainder of the passage
everything centers round the fact of His presence. The first part
shows the beginnings of a contest between forces apparently
human. The latter half depicts a struggle between the power of

God and that of antigod. In the present study we shall consider a number of these contrasts.

1. *The contrast between the man of the world and the man with faith* (vv. 1-16). As a typical man of the world, Goliath the giant defies the servants of the Living God. As a man of faith, the shepherd lad makes ready to fight for his country and his God. Between the two champions there can be no neutral ground. Neither will budge an inch before he conquers or falls. As often in an hour of crisis, hosts of passive bystanders watch every move in the conflict. Thus we have all the factors that enter into a drama.[1] Here we behold death-dealing action, heightened emotion, increasing suspense, and a tremendous climax—all in the style of a master painter.

First let us look at the typical militarist of the basest sort. Note how Goliath relies on bodily bigness. He depends on first-class equipment. He trusts in himself. Such an attitude of self-sufficiency seems to be as ancient as the human race. In recent times this spirit of insolent reliance on brute force appears to have experienced a rebirth. This pagan philosophy of life dominated our foes, both in Europe and in Asia. And has there been nothing of the sort here at home? The typical militarist acts much like Goliath. He trusts in himself, not in others; in things, not in God; in bigness, not in goodness; in the spirit of ruthless aggression, not in that of righteous activity. In short, he loves to fight. He lives to wage battle. He looks on war as his only god. Has such a spirit been growing in our midst of late?

By contrast the second paragraph of the story introduces a young man of God. This new champion of the Lord's people must have failed to impress them by his appearance. When he stood over against the giant, the stripling from the hills of Bethlehem must have looked puny. He lacked equipment for either

[1] See Fred Eastman, "The Dramatist and the Minister," chap. iv of *The Arts and Religion,* ed. Albert E. Bailey, Macmillan, 1944.

attack or defense. He could point to no experience as a warrior. Why, then, did he feel sure about the approaching triumph? Because he trusted in the Lord! According to the Apostle Paul, "God chose the weak things of the world, that he might put to shame the things that are strong." [2] For a living example, think of the Apostle himself.

This truth ought to hearten the Christian Church. The forces of God have always been outnumbered, just as they are today. Especially in recent years, the practical philosophy of Goliath has had its way the world over. Today the forces of bigness and bluff keep strutting up and down defying anyone who protests against their insolence. Would that we might discover a champion like young David! Such a man loves peace rather than war. He longs to build up, not to tear down. But when the people of God stand in peril because no one will champion their cause, he volunteers for the fray.

2. *The contrast between the older men who fear the foe and the young man who fights for God* (vv. 17-40). What caused the older men to fear the foe? Lack of faith! What inspired the young man's willingness to fight? Trust in the Lord! As we have often seen elsewhere, faith means that a man with human weakness lays hold of divine power and uses it in doing the will of God. In the unequal contest with Goliath, faith meant that a stripling looked to his Invisible King for wisdom and strength to accomplish what he never would have dreamed of attempting without divine support. The spirit of the young warrior resembled that of old John Knox. He feared God so much that he dreaded not the face of any mortal man, or even any woman.

Verses 17 to 27 show the weakness of us older men when we give way to fears. Like those passive bystanders of old, few of us claim to be saints. Even so, in a census of the community, or in a Gallup Poll, we should wish to be counted among "good

[2] I Cor. 1:27*b*.

church people." But we might pause to ask ourselves, "Good for what?" Do we not resemble King Saul and the older brothers of David? Evidently they had enrolled in the Do-Nothing Party. Why did not one of them go forth to slay that giant? Instead of attempting to impose unused armor on an inexperienced lad, why did not such a seasoned campaigner as King Saul gird up his loins and prepare for the conflict with that insolent giant? Because the "leader" had lost his faith! He had yielded to his fears. He had become as weak as water. Standing with him on the sidelines, far enough away to feel secure, a throng of shivering "warriors" waited for a shepherd lad to fight their battle.

Why did those veteran soldiers quail in the presence of a mere man? Doubtless they thought about the bigness of the giant and not about the greatness of their God. Thus far the record has scarcely alluded to the Almighty. The contrast between this first half of the narrative and the latter part reminds us of the difference between chapters 7 and 8 of Romans. In the latter part of the seventh chapter a man of mature years engages in a titanic struggle with his baser self. In fact, two men strive for the mastery of his soul. A noble Dr. Jekyll contends with a base Mr. Hyde. Much of the time Mr. Hyde seems likely to emerge the victor. But in the eighth chapter a complete change comes over the scene: the Holy Spirit takes control, God has His way in the heart, and soon it ceases to serve as a battlefield. Why should it not prove so whenever a man of God contends with demonic forces within his bosom?

The central portion of our narrative shows how a believer in God displays courage and resourcefulness. Without being asked, David volunteers to enter the lists against the giant. In the eyes of the country lad, Goliath must have looked almost as big as a mountain. And the sneers of David's elder brothers must have been hard to endure. Themselves too timid to fight, why did they try to dissuade their brother from entering the fray? Perhaps because of family pride. Did they wish to be publicly humiliated in the face of all their fellows? In passing we note the way the narrator brings out all these varieties of human reaction. Simply from the viewpoint of literary composition, the passage would merit our study. However, let us keep to religion.

Why did that young shepherd trust God on the field of battle? Because of his previous experiences back on the hills of home. Among his beloved sheep he had gained strength and skill to slay a lion and a bear. Some such experiences must have led the ancients to devise the legend of Antaeus. According to the chronicles of old, that giant wrestler of Libya seemed invincible. Whenever his body touched mother earth, he would receive fresh infusions of strength. What that legend tells about mother earth, young David found true of his God. From Him through faith the young warrior received courage and strength to conquer the giant. With Tennyson the young shepherd might have sung:

My strength is as the strength of ten,
Because my heart is pure.

This hero of faith dared to fight in his own way. Back on the hills near Bethlehem he had relied on no cumbersome armor and equipment, and yet he had slain more than one wild beast. In the new crisis, also, he insisted on thinking and acting for himself. He made his own choice of weapons, and he used all the skill he had gained as a shepherd. Thus he stood out in contrast with Saul. Why did the older man strive to put on young David the armor that the king was too cowardly to wear? Perhaps because the ruler had yielded to the contagion of depending on things rather than on God. The younger man must have known that the Lord wished everyone to be himself, his very best self.

Here one is tempted to turn aside and deliver a homily on "The Duty of Being Yourself." Among all the temptations of us older folks, what can be more subtle than that of imposing our ways on young people? How many of earth's giants have we older folks slain? Scarcely a one! Run down through the list! Think of militarism, secularism, race prejudice, commercialized vice, the liquor traffic, and other massive evils before which we quail and accept defeat without a fight. Today every one of those giant evils struts up and down before us church folk, defying us to our faces. When some young man volunteers to slay such a giant, do we bid him welcome and Godspeed? Rather do we not greet him with sneers like those of David's elder brothers?

Surely the young leader of tomorrow can fail no more dismally than we have done. How then can he solve our problems and slay our giants, one by one? Not by putting on the unused armor of some older man! Why does it look so new and bright? Because it has never gone into battle to be pierced and warped. All this and more comes out of the biblical narrative. But where we indulge in sweeping plurals, the Book leads us to behold one shepherd lad as he goes out to slay a single giant. Who but a man of faith would dare to depend on a slingshot and five stones from the brook? In the difficult days that lie ahead, let every young man fight for God in a way all his own. Let every David be himself!

An object lesson comes from a recent book. A worker among rural mountain folk in central Missouri found there two evils strongly intrenched. He had to contend with illegal making of whiskey and with blood feuds. The young "shepherd of the hills" fought those two giant evils in a fashion all his own. In an hour of crisis he gained strength from the assurance of a mountain woman: "We'll be praying the good Lord helps you find the right stone to slay Goliath. Corn liquor is the giant enemy of these hills."[3] Ere long the opportunity came—at the funeral of a lad who had been killed by rotgut whiskey.

[3] Guy Howard, *Walkin' Preacher of the Ozarks* (Harper, 1944), p. 155. (Because of this book the preacher has had to leave the field!)

How was the young parson able to avert a blood feud and stop the making of moonshine whiskey? How could he fulfill the desire of the boy's mother when she cried: "If hit only saves some other mother's boy from drink I'll know John didn't die fer nothin'"? Near the end of the funeral address the preacher implored all the "good people" to stop making whiskey illegally at home. He also insisted that they drive out the few men who manufactured illicit liquor for sale. In both these endeavors he appears to have succeeded.

One of the better mountaineers told him why they were smashing their stills: "I've made a little liquor all along fur my own use, . . . but I'm shore goin' home and bust up my still even if it war Pap's. I don't never 'low to make ary use of hit. They's others agoin' to do the same fer we'uns jist figgered hit wouldn't be much use fightin' somethin' we'uns doin' ourselves."[4]

Elsewhere one of those mountain friends struck down to the root of the matter: "Only thing thet'll make a man quit drinkin', cussin', and all his other orneriness is ter give him a big dose of God. . . . And I reckon yo're gettin' a purty good start fixin' up the medicine. If we'uns keep aworkin' and aprayin' we'uns jest naturally bound ter git some of 'em cured, showin' 'em the grace of a lovin', fergivin' Lord."[5]

3. *The contrast between the warrior who relies on self and the one who trusts in God* (vv. 41-49). Here the drama reaches a climax. The words of the ancient writer present the facts so strongly and sharply that one should read them aloud. Then he will note the contrast between the boastfulness of the giant and the bravery of the stripling. There struts the big bully from Bragtown. Who can hope to slay such a colossus encased in armor? If anyone there had been foolhardy enough to bet on the

---

[4] *Ibid.,* p. 160.
[5] *Ibid.,* pp. 144-45.

outcome, he would have heard all the "experts" predicting the defeat of the challenger.

On the other hand, every impartial observer would have wished to see the stripling win. Look at his poise and his assurance. Listen to his words as he addresses the giant: "Thou comest to me with a sword, and with a spear, and with a javelin: but I come to thee in the name of the Lord of hosts, the God of the armies of Israel, whom thou hast defied. This day will the Lord deliver thee into my hands!" Truly, "this is the victory that hath overcome the world, even our faith." [6]

The young man appears to be fully as confident as the giant. If David had gone into that contest expecting to be defeated and slain, doubtless he would have fallen before the giant's sword. But by faith the champion of Israel must have known that it was not the will of the Lord for the Philistine to prevail. Today we often refer to belief in "the sovereignty of God." Whatever we call the truth, our hope for a better world rests in the goodness and the might of our Invisible King.

As long as David lived he could look back on that scene. In his mind's eye he could behold the giant strutting back and forth with insolent disdain for those shivering "children of God." The former shepherd lad could likewise recall the later spectacle of the dead giant stretched out upon the sand. What a silent symbol of the doom that will someday befall the forces of evil in a world where God will have His way!

4. *The contrast between the fleeing foe and the man of faith* (vv. 45-58). In order to make the situation clear let us recall the terms of the contest, which from our point of view seem passing strange. If the champion of the Israelites could slay the giant, then the invading Philistines would lay down their arms. They would even become the slaves of the conquerors. But if Goliath prevailed, the Israelites were to be enslaved. That weird proposal

[6] I John 5:4b.

came from the giant. How did his people carry out their part of the contract?

As soon as they saw the giant fall, the Philistines fled. When have the forces of evil kept their word of honor? Only when by so doing they could advance their nefarious schemes. After the repeal of prohibition, for instance, the liquor traffic made all sorts of promises, voluntarily. How many of those beautiful pledges has the rum traffic tried to carry out? Not a one! On the contrary, the business has become so solidly entrenched that it even defies the Church. Who will dare to oppose this giant evil that stands ready to enslave our sons and daughters?

By way of contrast look at young David. Note the humility of the young hero. Why does he wear his new laurels modestly? He knows that the victory has come from the hands of God. In like manner Albert Einstein once told a friend who had referred to the scientist as "great": "I have nothing that I have not received!" With Abraham Lincoln let us repeat, "Oh, why should the spirit of mortal be proud?" And with the psalmist let us pray, "Not unto us, O Lord, not unto us, but unto thy name give glory!" [7]

The triumph over Goliath marked a turning point in the career of young David. By this feat he captured the hearts of the common people and appealed to the popular imagination. Henceforth for years he would stand as the embodiment of their ideals: courage and modesty, unselfishness and generosity. At the same time King Saul had shown his inability to rule. Had he not displayed cowardice in the face of the enemy, and unwillingness to lead in the hour of crisis?

That day witnessed the beginning of Saul's antipathy for David. From that time onward the king, as the Scriptures say, "eyed" the young favorite whose praises were being sung throughout the land. All the while the young hero kept his heart

[7] Psa. 115:1a.

unspoiled. Like young Joseph in Egypt after he had suddenly been elevated to high office, David kept on doing well whatever came to his hand. Thus he set before the people an ideal of stalwart young manhood. To this very hour he has much to teach the followers of Christ.

All this while someone may have wished to ask: "What has David's exploit to do with me?" That depends on the will of the Lord for you personally. Does He wish you to become a leader of men? If so, He would have you emulate the spirit of this young champion. For a concrete symbol of David's spirit look at the giant's sword. After the victory over Goliath, young David put that trophy away in the house of the Lord. There he wished it to serve as a token of God's power to deliver His people in the day of peril. Later, in a time of desperate need, David took that sword out of the temple and with it extricated himself from danger.[8]

These facts led Horace Bushnell to deliver a message that deserves to be well known. With the topic "The Best Weapons Gotten by Conquest," the strongest of our American pulpit masters spoke on the proposition: "There is no so good weapon for a Christian as that which he has gotten by his own personal victories." In other words, "Each victory will help you some other to win." Have you laid up in the temple of your heart the recollection of a sword wrested from the hand of a deadly enemy? If so, rest assured that in some hour of dire need you can take down the very same weapon and with it gain another victory for King Jesus.

These are excerpts and echoes from Bushnell's sermon: The whole of the Christian life is a warfare. The soldier is to gain power by his victories. Observe the importance to the Christian of making first victories. You will be vanquished everywhere if you do not begin to vanquish somewhere. The difficulty with most

[8] I Sam. 21:9.

Christians is that they endeavor to gain a general victory, and no victory in particular. God has not enlisted us for defeat. Come, now, here is the sword you wait for. You can even touch it with your fingers. Take it, and it is yours. And then, success and victory to the end! [9]

Phillips Brooks, the most beloved of American divines, has left us much the same message. Under the heading "The Egyptians Dead upon the Seashore," he assures us that "nothing which ought not to be need be." Listen to the closing words of his moving sermon:

Get something done! Do not go on forever in idle skirmishing with the same foe. Realize, as you sit here, who your enemy is, what vice of mind or body, what false or foul habit. Cry out to God for strength. Set your face resolutely to a new life in which that vice shall have no part. Go out and leave it dead. Plenty of new battles and new foes, but no longer that battle and that foe! Get something done! May He who overcame, not merely for Himself, but for us all, give you courage and make you sharers in His victory, and in the liberty which He attained.[10]

In view of such discourses think of that oft-repeated question: "How can I preach from the Old Testament?" Instead of dealing with the matter abstractly, why not study Bushnell and Brooks? Remember that neither of them would be counted an old fogy today. And yet each of them went repeatedly to the Hebrew Bible and found there many a message that struck home to the heart, the conscience, and the will. Who follows in that train?

---

[9] See *The Spirit in Man* (Scribner, 1903), pp. 103-19.
[10] *Sermons*, VI, 55-72.

THE HEIGHT OF HUMAN FRIENDSHIP

1 Samuel 18 and 20

FROM THIS POINT ONWARD WE SHALL DEAL WITH BIBLE CHAPTERS here and there. To take up every passage would call for much time and space. Just now we are to think about Jonathan, the son of King Saul. Since the facts about Jonathan appear more simply in chapter 18 than in chapter 20, we shall think only about the earlier passage. The crown prince has become famous largely because of his friendship with David, but the king's son deserved to be known in his own right. Indeed, he may have been responsible for much of the goodness in the younger man. As long as Jonathan lived to befriend him, David went on in the path of honor. After Jonathan died, the other man fell into gross sins. At present, however, the two concern us as examples of human friendship at its height.

Friendship differs from friendliness. As the term is here employed, friendship refers to the sort of intimate relationship that comes to a strong man only once or twice in his earthly career. On the other hand, friendliness reaches out to include everybody. Instead of dealing with the matter theoretically, let us think of a modern example. Phillips Brooks, the most beloved pastor of our time, seems to have had only a few bosom friends. Those he selected with exceeding care. But he showed himself friendly with all sorts of human beings, from young Helen Keller to the august president of Harvard University. At the same time Brooks showed the people of his day the meaning of Shakespeare's familiar lines from *Hamlet:*

Be thou familiar, but by no means vulgar;
The friends thou hast, and their adoption tried,
Grapple them to thy soul with hoops of steel.

1. *The beauty of human friendship* (I Sam. 18:1-5). "The soul of Jonathan was knit with the soul of David." The figure of speech suggests the weaving of a pattern day after day. The process calls for skill and care as well as love and zeal. To the weaving of this friendship Jonathan must have devoted hours of time as well as loving care. Since he was the older of the two, as well as the crown prince, he took the first steps; and he followed them with many others. From young David the prince met with a hearty response. The two of them had evidently been made for each other. Their friendship has given us a pattern by which we measure other examples of love between man and man.[1]

Our passage likewise speaks of human friendship in terms of a covenant: "Jonathan and David made a covenant, because he loved him as his own soul." In Old Testament days the people of God attached untold importance to the idea of a covenant. If we used words accurately, we should speak of the Old Testament as the Old Covenant. We find this use of the word in the American Revised Version, which puts on a title page: "The New Covenant, commonly called The New Testament." In the Holy Communion, also, when the clergyman declares, on behalf of his Lord, "This cup is the New Testament in my blood," the words really mean "The New Covenant."

In these two cases the word "covenant" relates to God and men. It refers to His grace in choosing us as His children, and to our faith in accepting Him as our Father. This way of looking at religion has met with special favor among church folk in Scotland and in the Netherlands. In 1638 and again in 1641 our

---

[1] For another example see the closing pages of Charles Dickens' *The Tale of Two Cities;* also read in Roman history about Damon and Pythias.

Scottish forefathers at Edinburgh signed and sealed the Covenant. At old Greyfriars Churchyard some of them are said to have done so with blood drawn from their veins. They found no difficulty in thinking about religion as a covenant. In fact, they often looked on Jonathan as a type of the coming Redeemer. To us that may seem farfetched. At least we find in the New Testament no warrant for thinking of Jonathan in terms of Jesus Christ. Still we can see a resemblance between the Hebrew prince and our King of Kings.

What then do we understand by a covenant between man and man? By way of analogy let us think of marriage. In a well-known ceremony the clergyman speaks to the contracting parties about "the covenant between you made." In still another realm we refer to a covenant as binding nations. After World War I we heard much about the "covenant" in the Treaty of Peace. Now that we are thinking more and more about Latin America we long to see the Christ of the Andes. Even at a distance we know that Chile and Argentina almost went to war, and that they celebrated the covenant of peace by erecting a massive statue with the inscription: "Sooner shall these mountains crumble to dust than Chile and Argentina shall break the peace they have sworn at the feet of the Redeemer."

We conclude that a covenant relates to a solemn agreement between two persons, or it may be two parties. When the covenant has to do with friendship between man and man we infer that each of them has declared his undying devotion to the other, and that they have bound their hearts together with ties of loyalty as well as love. What a beautiful conception of human friendship!

2. *The antithesis of human friendship* (I Sam. 18:6-16). The contrasting spirit to friendship is envy. Envy has long held its place among the seven deadly sins. Envy took a leading role among "the sins that crucified Jesus." Even pagan Pilate "knew that for envy they had delivered him up." To this day envy works

more havoc than certain spectacular sins, such as gambling. And yet one seldom preaches about the ravages wrought by envy. All unconsciously, one may hesitate to speak of the evil spirit that possesses the soul of the prominent layman, or it may be his wife. Even the minister is not immune.

As with a cancer in the breast, envy eats into the tissues of the soul, and may even cause speedy death. For an object lesson of envy's power to consume the soul, look at King Saul. Go out among his most loyal subjects. Hear them as they murmur to one another: "What has come over our king? Once he set our sons an example of strength and courage. Now he seems possessed with jealousy and fear. Why has he become a baser man?" They never suspected him of playing the hypocrite. They always felt that he was sincere. Gradually they must have seen how envy had become an obsession which was eating away his soul.

Such a spectacle reminds us that the beginnings of envy may be small and apparently harmless. "Saul eyed David." What a verb! With what venom does envy eye its victim. If looks could slay, few men like David would survive. What causes this evil spirit to spring up within the heart? In the parlance of sophisticated folk, envy may be only the "manifestation of an inferiority complex." Whatever the attempted explanation in psychological terminology, envy keeps working untold havoc, both within the soul and out in the world. Unless held back by forces still mightier, this evil spirit may lead a man to break all the Ten Commandments and to ignore the Cross of Christ.

Envy often means the coveting of another person's charm or his good fortune. Such a way of looking up with spite indicates that the other person must be superior. Who ever felt jealous of another man because of his weakness or his failure? In the realm of character or achievement the envied person must have risen to heights of which the envier has only dreamed. Since the victim of jealousy and spite cannot hope to climb that steep ascent, why must he strive to drag the other person down? What a sorry place our world would become if no one excelled any of us in goodness and strength!

The facts about Saul likewise show that the growth of this evil spirit may be rapid. At first the envier contents himself with baleful looks. Then he becomes obsessed with baseless fears. Erelong he imagines himself the victim of diabolical plots. Sooner or later he voices bitter feelings in words that scald and sear. At length he resorts to violent deeds. What a descent from the modesty and charm of young Saul to the caprice and cruelty of a killer King! When has a cancer ever eaten into the body more quickly than envy consumed this man's soul?

One more stage is left and only one. Unless it be checked, this evil spirit will soon prove fatal. Unless the cancer be taken out of the soul, or the growth retarded, the life of the victim will end in tragedy. With Saul what began as an intermittent disorder resolved itself into an abiding obsession—an obsession which in time led to his death. With him fell the dynasty that had only begun. In his collapse he caused the whole nation to suffer, even while it mourned. What a mighty epidemic of evil may issue from envy within a single breast!

Is there any cure for this deadly disease? Find the answer in religion. Study the records about young Jonathan. From him learn how to ward off the insidious attacks of envy. Note how love within the soul exorcises this evil spirit. Love for God leads a young man like Jonathan to be patient and kind with his erratic father. The same loving spirit prompts young David to forgive the king who has done him deadly wrong. To the present hour who among us has ever envied a man whom he loved? By the grace of God any of us can reach the level where he thanks the Lord for the goodness, the charm, and the influence of that other person. In the golden age when this spirit of love is to prevail throughout the world, wars will be no more.

In our own days of reconstruction we need to study the attitude of Jonathan toward David. If King Saul had an excuse for feeling envious of the shepherd lad from the hills, how much more had the crown prince! Did he not know that the younger man seemed destined to receive the crown which would otherwise have gone to Jonathan? On the other hand, the religion of Jonathan served as a sort of antitoxin to ward off every attack of envy. When will the Christian Church begin to carry this sort of prophylaxis to the nations of the earth?

If we look back over the last few pages we shall note the contrast between the beauty of friendship and the ugliness of envy. We may even think of religion as a deepening friendship between God and men. In a still higher form we can learn this truth from our Master: "No longer do I call you servants; for the servant knoweth not what his lord doeth: but I have called you friends." [2] Better still, He is waiting to transform the spirit of envy into feelings of love. Surely this brings us close to the heart of all the mystery known as "personal religion." [3]

The spirit of true religion appears in a tale of olden times. With his wife and children, Tigranes the king of Armenia had been taken captive. Soon they were led before Pompey to receive the sentence of death. In that royal presence Tigranes pleaded that he alone might suffer, and that his dear ones might go free. That spirit of self-sacrificing love so moved the heart of Pompey that he ordered the release of the entire household. On their homeward way Tigranes said to his wife, "What did you think of the Emperor?"

"Indeed, I never saw him!"

"You never saw Pompey? Where were your eyes?"

"They were fixed upon the one who offered to die for me!"

[2] John 15:15.
[3] See Douglas C. Macintosh's informing *Personal Religion*, Scribner, 1942.

144

CHAPTER 19

THE FORGIVENESS OF DEADLY WRONGS

I Samuel 24 and 26

EVERY WAR RAISES AN ENDLESS SERIES OF PROBLEMS ABOUT THE forgiveness of deadly wrongs. Ofttimes the period of so-called reconstruction intensifies and prolongs the spirit of reprisal. Was it not so during the years that followed 1861-65, as well as after 1914-18? In view of carefully authenticated reports of atrocities by our foes in World War II, both in Europe and in the Pacific, should the victorious powers wreak vengeance? No more serious problem in religion and ethics faces the "Christian" world.

How shall the man in the pulpit meet this vital issue? He will ever find it hard to preach about ethics, and never more so than now. Instead of dealing with the matter abstractly, why not study an actual case? Let it be as simple as possible, if it presents the issue squarely. Where can you find a better example than in the facts about young David's forgiveness of King Saul? Since the facts in chapter 24 resemble those in chapter 26, we shall think only about the former passage. All the while let us remember that such a man has to forgive more than once. In fact, he may do so "until seventy times seven." [1]

1. *The meaning of forgiveness* (I Sam. 24:1-7). "A wrong" means a serious injury, or an offense, committed by one person against another. Sometimes a million or more heap insults and abuses on the heads of countless other people. For the sake of simplicity and clearness, however, we shall watch a single person on either side. We shall assume that the innocent party

[1] Matt. 18:22.

has done nothing to provoke acts of aggression. We shall likewise take for granted that the offense concerns life and honor. As for petty pin pricks which wound a man's vanity, why do we not accept them as a matter of course, much as we do with gnats on an evening in August? Now we are to face the problem of a strong king's trying to kill the young follower who has shown him nothing but loyal devotion.

The deed of King Saul constituted a sin against God. It likewise involved a crime against the State. These distinctions loom large, because the person who suffers the injury must be the one who forgives the wrong. A man sins against God. Hence David is said to have sung:

> Against thee, thee only, have I sinned,
> And done that which is evil in thy sight.[2]

The same offense constitutes a crime against the government. The physical injury may fall on a defenseless mortal. In like manner, the person who has suffered must do the pardoning. God alone can forgive a sin; the government alone can pardon a crime; the injured party alone can forgive a wrong.

What principle undergirds all these facts? Simply this: a man's forgiveness of deadly wrongs ought to be like God's forgiveness of that man's sins. Really one forgives the person, not the injury, but still one speaks about "forgiveness of wrongs." Such an act calls for more than pardon. According to a recent book that every pastor should use daily, "one pardons when one frees from the penalty due for an offense or refrains from exacting punishment," and "one forgives when one gives up not only any claim to requital or retribution, but also any resentment or desire for revenge."[3] What a lofty ideal! For an example turn to Lord

[2] Psa. 51:4a.

[3] *Webster's Dictionary of Synonymns* (Merriam, 1942), p. 312b.

THE FORGIVENESS OF DEADLY WRONGS

Tennyson's *Idylls of the King*. Arthur is speaking to Queen Guinevere, who has done him the deadliest of wrongs:

> Well is it that no child is born of thee.
> The children born of thee are sword and fire,
> Red ruin, and the breaking up of laws.
>
> . . . .
>
> And all is past, the sin is sinn'd, and I,
> Lo! I forgive thee, as Eternal God
> Forgives: do thou for thine own soul the rest.

For a still nobler example read the Book of Hosea.

Now let us turn directly to our case. King Saul strove to murder young David. At least twice the latter forgave that deadly wrong. For a parallel case turn to Joseph back in Genesis.[4] He could never forget that his elder brothers had envied and hated him, that they had wanted to kill him, and that they had sold him into bondage. After thirteen years of hardship as a slave in Egypt, Joseph became practically the ruler of the land. Then he went far out of his way to forgive those who had done him the deadliest wrongs. Not only did he take the first step to bring about a reconciliation with those brothers; he did everything else in his power to win the love of the men who had inflicted on him the bitterest of mortal injuries. In his case, as with David, the forgiving spirit seems to have sprung from religion. In like manner David exclaimed: "The Lord forbid that I should do this thing unto my lord, the Lord's anointed, to put forth my hand against him, seeing he is the Lord's anointed."

2. *The practical workings of forgiveness* (I Sam. 24:8-15). Remember that forgiveness of wrongs means restoring the offender to the place he would have occupied in one's heart if he had not inflicted the injury. Behold young David sparing the life of the one man on earth whom it must have proved hardest

---

[4] Study with care Gen. 45:1-15 and Gen. 50:15-21.

to forgive. What kind of treatment had the shepherd youth a right to expect from his king? Justice, as well as kindness, with gratitude for valiant services gladly rendered. As the ruler of the land King Saul ought to have hazarded his life for the sake of any young man in the kingdom. Most of all did the monarch owe a lasting debt to young David. And yet the latter forgave! Who is the hardest person on earth to pardon? The one whom you have most loved and best served. When that man turns against you, and does you deadly wrongs, wholly without cause, only the grace of God can hold you back from a desire for vengeance.

Herein lies the most searching test of a man's religion. It demands that he forgive, if need be, again and again. At Engedi, on the western bank of the Dead Sea, young David let King Saul go unharmed. At Ziph, about sixteen miles westward among the hills, again the younger man spared the life of his king. Each time David must have known that he was exposing himself to the deadliest peril. How could he hope to survive when he was being hunted like a partridge on the mountains? Doubtless he committed himself into the hands of God, who alone could impart the grace to forgive.

The goodness of God leads a man to forgive the deadliest of wrongs. In other words, doctrine undergirds duty. If we seem to be looking at Hebrew history in the light of the Cross, that is the way for us Christians to study the Old Testament. What else do we mean when we pray: "Forgive us our trespasses as we forgive those that trespass against us"? What a lofty standard for sinful mortals! If Joseph and David acted according to such a "counsel of perfection," how much more should we who dwell on the Christian side of Calvary? Do we not hear our Saviour calling: "Father, forgive them; for they know not what they do"? [5]

The spirit of Christian forgiveness appears in unexpected

[5] Luke 23:34a.

places, even in politics. In 1884, when Grover Cleveland was running for the presidency, his opponents dug out of his past the ugliest and blackest of facts. Though he had striven to right those wrongs of a misspent youth, he manfully accepted the odium. Erelong his supporters brought to the executive mansion at Albany documents proving that his opponent's early record had been equally shameful. Cleveland read the papers through with care. Then he asked: "Gentlemen, are these documents mine, to use as I think best?" Receiving an affirmative reply, he walked over to the fireplace and threw the incriminating evidence on the burning coals. Then he said quietly: "The other side can have a monopoly of the mud in this campaign."

In our American politics, neither side has had any monopoly of mud or of morals. Soon after William McKinley was elected governor of Ohio one of his closest advisers asked whom he intended to appoint for a certain important office. When McKinley mentioned a certain man, the adviser protested: "Surely you know that he did everything in his power to prevent your becoming Governor. Why honor a bitter opponent?" "I know all of that, but still I feel that he is the best man in Ohio for this particular office." Then McKinley added, with his disarming smile: "If we spend all our time getting even, we shall never get ahead." Can you wonder that McKinley and Cleveland, with all their contrasting traits, respected and liked each other? Would that such old-fashioned gallantry had obtained in some of our recent contests for the presidency.

3. *The response to forgiveness of wrongs* (I Sam. 24:16-22). Before it can be complete, forgiveness must be accepted. This holds true between man and man as surely as between man and God. The Lord stands ready to pardon everyone who has done Him deadly wrongs. As our Invisible King, He holds out the scepter of mercy. By His Spirit, He says to His sinful children: "Be ye reconciled to God." But—we confess it to our shame—

149

many of us do not accept His proffered mercy. So it seems to have been with King Saul. When first he learned about young David's magnanimity in sparing the king's life, the ruler "lifted up his voice, and wept." But before many days had passed, the very same "penitent" was out on the hills trying to run down and slay innocent David. Even so, the young man kept on loving the implacable king!

Ideally, the forgiving spirit would lead to a change of attitude on the part of the other person. As any pastor can bear witness, earth's noblest friendship may spring up between two men who have become reconciled through forgiveness of wrongs. Would that the same principle of grace might begin to operate among the powers that were recently at war. Instead of the spirit that led Shylock to demand a pound of flesh close to the heart, let the conquering nations devise conditions of peace that embody justice tempered with mercy. Then may the vanquished peoples respond in the spirit of brotherly love. All of that might help to usher in what William James used to term "the moral equivalent of war."

The same principle of "malice toward none" ought to govern all our dealings with people of other races. Not long after Pearl Harbor we herded thousands of Japanese Americans into relocation camps. There we caused them to suffer indignities untold. Even so, we have found in many of them no evidence of resentment. If such a spirit of ruthlessness is to mark our dealings with our former foes, how can we hope for aught save resentment and desire for reprisal? As long as the peoples of earth treat each other like wild beasts, how can we hope to escape from war after war? That may have been one reason why Abraham Lincoln spent his last days in devising honorable ways of bringing the Southern states back into the Union. If he had lived to carry out his plans, we might never have witnessed the shameful debaucheries of so-called reconstruction days. How do we plan to "reconstruct" the lands we conquered during World War II?

THE FORGIVENESS OF DEADLY WRONGS

Many of us private citizens keep wondering what we can do to promote peace among the nations. At least we can pray that the Spirit of Christ may lead and restrain those who sit in high places and there help to determine the history of tomorrow. We can likewise resolve that by God's grace we shall deal justly and kindly with all our neighbors, especially with those of other races and tongues. While we continue to send out missionaries for Asia and Africa, let us also make our homeland a safe and a happy abode for all our minority groups.

Two current examples of brotherhood come to mind. One concerns a group of Mexican laborers on the railroad. For over two years these 350 "day hands" have made their temporary home at Plainsboro, N. J. During the entire time they have caused no disturbance in the community. Their record with the Pennsylvania Railroad has been better than that of any similar group elsewhere. The officials of the company ascribe practically all the credit to the church people of this community. Especially active have been a number of our Spanish-speaking students at the Seminary. What have they done? They have simply treated these "strangers within our midst" as though they were normal human beings. Surely we owe far more than that to people from Mexico!

The same spirit may rule between members of the white race and their Negro neighbors. After years of residence in the South, the writer feels that his Negro friends are safe in the keeping of the many Caucasian Christians whom he knows and loves in that part of the land. Unfortunately, not all of the white folk there or here have caught the spirit of the Master in dealing with members of the Negro race. Consequently, race prejudice appears to be spreading, in both the South and the North. Such unchristian feelings appear to be still more intense over in South Africa. Race prejudice breeds world-wide wars.

What can we do? Every white person can live in the spirit of the Golden Rule. A recent experience shows how it works. At an interracial conference a brilliant young Negro leader was expected to act as a firebrand. On the contrary, he proved to be most friendly and anxious to co-operate. In the course of the meetings he explained his change of attitude. On a distant city thoroughfare he had accidentally passed between a white lady and her gentleman escort. The Negro felt dismayed, for he knew that he had committed an unpardonable offense. Before he could frame an abject apology the white gentleman removed his hat, bowed, and expressed regret for the embarrassment. He insisted that he alone had been to blame. "Love suffereth long, and is kind."

Think what a passing stranger had done in a minute to promote good will between these two groups, each suspicious of the other. Why does such an incident seem rare enough to receive comment? For further light on the whole problem turn to Edwin R. Embree, president of the Julius Rosenwald Foundation, who has written a most interesting account of representative Negro leaders in the United States.[6] These men and women fall into two groups: those who feel kindly toward us white folk; and those who seem bitter. With few exceptions those who feel kindly have met with the right sort of Caucasian Christians. Those who seem bitter have encountered the opposite. At heart, therefore, as with every other problem, this one comes back to the individual. Why not be kind to every Negro you meet? Then the "problem" may become an opportunity.

This matter of forgiving wrongs calls for teaching by the minister. At one of the "Bible conferences" where one is supposed to interpret the Scriptures, the author was discussing the practical workings of forgiveness. Afterward one of the prominent women

[6] See *Thirteen Against the Odds,* Viking, 1944; also *What the Negro Wants,* ed. Rayford W. Logan, University of North Carolina Press, 1945.

in that part of the land said to him privately: "I am glad that you are not my pastor!"

"Please tell me why."

"Because you make it hard to live as a Christian!"

"Pardon me, madam, I simply interpret what I find in the Scriptures, especially in the teachings of our Lord."

"Ah, that's the rub! It hurts me to find how far I fall short of being a Christian!"

That good woman needed to sit at the feet of a teaching minister. Then she would have understood what Alexander Duff used to say about his work in India: "The first business of the missionary is to create a conscience; . . . a man without a conscience is a man without a character." Such a conviction grows out of the fact that the Bible tells as much about duty as about doctrine. The Scriptures contain as many precepts as promises. Who will volunteer to interpret what the Book says about this difficult duty? Why not begin with David's forgiveness of Saul?

CHAPTER 20

THE INFLUENCE OF A WOMAN'S CHARM

I Samuel 25

AGAIN WE ARE TO ENGAGE IN A STUDY OF CONTRASTS. THROUGHOUT chapters 24 and 26 of First Samuel we stand in the presence of envy, wrath, and attempted murder. Between these two passages we find a different sort of narrative. Here, too, we look upon a rough and ruthless era, a sort of hangover from the time of the Judges. We must watch the unbridled passions of bloodthirsty warriors. In their midst we soon descry a dainty, charming woman, courageously intervening to avert needless bloodshed. Thus we have our materials for study of a good woman's charm.

What do we mean by charm? According to one of Sir James M. Barrie's heroines, it is "a sort of bloom on a woman. If you have it, you don't need to have anything else, and if you don't have it, it doesn't matter much what else you have." For a living object lesson, study Abigail. Let her call to mind the words of Ruskin: "The soul's armor is never well set to the heart unless a woman's hand has braced it, and it is only when she braces it lightly that the honor of manhood fails." So let us see how a good woman wields her spell over an angry warrior bent on shedding blood.

1. *The sort of man a good woman should not marry* (vv. 1-17). This wife and her husband, Abigail and Nabal, might have sat for a series of satirical paintings by some old-time Hogarth. If so, the title might have been "Marriage à la Mode," or else "Beauty and the Beast." The husband's name means "foolish," "reckless," or "churlish." The word "churl" sets him off as a burly brute

with a growl and a snarl like an angry mastiff ready to bite. And yet that churl possessed a farm and a fortune, both of which he may have inherited from a thrifty father. With all of that wealth the churl showed ingratitude toward a warrior who had done him good, insolence toward one who might work him harm, and brutality to everybody he could intimidate. You see the type! Over against him look at Boaz, a noble country gentleman who deserved to become the husband of another charming woman, even Ruth.[1] Think of Nabal and Boaz as well-to-do farmers in that same bloody era.

Why should a charming young woman have married such a brute as Nabal? She must have watched him begin to grow old long before his time. Perhaps she expected to have him reform. More probably her parents had yielded to the lure of his gold. What will an ambitious mother not accept in the way of a son-in-law if he possesses a landed estate and a bank account! The dear matron may assure her husband that they have handsomely provided for their daughter. But if those parents live long after the wedding they will see that her only hope of happiness lies in the prospect of his speedy demise. Thus the chapter might lead us to a study of marriage, with all its ideals and its perils.

2. *The sort of woman a good man should wed* (vv. 18-22). For a more detailed study of a good woman's charm turn to the acrostic poem in the thirty-first chapter of Proverbs. Read also the thirty-first chapter of Job, with its full-length picture of a noble man. These two passages bring into bold relief the virtues the Hebrews prized in their country people. In First Samuel the good woman's attractions appear in deeds rather than words. Even so, if we listen to what little she says we can learn much about the practical workings of a good woman's charm.

This one had all the gifts and graces that she would require when she became a queen. She possessed a good understanding.

[1] See Ruth 2:4, and page 176.

Probably she never let the man in her home discover her superior ability. She must have known that her husband would not wish to be overshadowed. She likewise had beauty of person, and ability to win the love of others, high or low. She had captured the hearts of the servants on the farm, so that they confided in her when they dared not approach their churlish master. Such winsomeness still flourishes in many a home. What Emerson once wrote still holds true: "America excels in women."

What has all this to do with religion? Much, in every way! Do not the Scriptures teach us to look on the right sort of home as the most important spot in all our world? Under God, does not the making of such a heaven on earth depend chiefly upon the wife and mother? If the households of our country had enough good women like Abigail, each with a husband worthy to be the father of her children, we could rear a generation of strong leaders for Church and State. What nobler service can we Bible teachers render than that of nurturing young women and girls such as Abigail? Without knowing the facts, one dares to surmise that she grew to womanhood under the friendly eye of an older woman with charm, and under the tutelage of a mature man full of grace and truth. Now let us behold Abigail in action.

3. *How a good woman makes the best of a sorry mess* (vv. 23-31). When peril drew near and threatened to sweep away her all, Abigail might have folded her hands and said with a sigh: "I am not to blame! Let matters take their course!" Instead, she sprang up and acted with a daring like that of Queen Esther.[2] Each of those charming women must have known that she had come on the scene for an hour of crisis. In each case the means of averting disaster proved to be feminine. Without becoming weak and sentimental, each of them kept on being her own sweet, gracious self. Each had learned how to get along with a rash and powerful man intent on shedding blood wholesale. Instead

[2] See Esther 4:16.

of risking a direct frontal attack on David, the infuriated warrior, Abigail resorted to what we term a "psychological approach." That called for meeting the angry man on his own ground, and for leading him to alter his course of action. How a good woman can wield such charm, who can tell? Let us watch her every move.

Behold her humility. She knows that David and his young troopers are swooping down on the farmstead, bent on slaying all its inmates. Bidding one of the servants saddle an ass, she rides out to meet the angry war lord and his band. When she catches sight of the coming troops she alights from her beast and prostrates herself in the roadway. As soon as David rides up she accosts him, almost abjectly. Four times in quick succession she addresses him as "my lord." How else could she have moved the heart of that outraged leader so surely as by acknowledging the justice of his cause?

Likewise consider her tact. Amid all the haste of her departure, she has taken time to bring an abundance of food. She has realized that those advancing soldiers would be half starved, and has known that their fury would abate when they had been fed. Discreetly she says that she has brought nourishment for the young men, but she does not include David. She knows that he too must be almost beside himself with hunger; still she speaks as to a practical idealist who is intent on doing the will of God. After she has won her way into his heart she can utter words that would have made him wince if she had spoken them first.

Listen now as she appeals to the warrior's faith in God: "Forgive, I pray thee, the trespass of thy handmaid: for the Lord will certainly make my lord a sure house, because my lord fighteth the battles of the Lord; and evil shall not be found in thee all thy days." Then follows her assurance that David will triumph over his foes because he trusts in God. How could she have voiced a more effective plea to a servant of the Most High, to a warrior who had for the time forgotten his religion?

Then follows an appeal to the strong man's conscience. She bids him look onward to the day when he shall commence to rule over the land. In that glad hour will he wish to recall the massacre that he now threatens to commit? For such another moving appeal to heart and conscience turn to the forty-fourth chapter of Genesis. There Judah pleads for the life and the freedom of his younger brother Benjamin. For another object lesson read *The Heart of Midlothian,* by Sir Walter Scott. There a country lass named Jeanie Deans appears before Queen Caroline to beg for the life of Effie Deans. This younger sister has "loved not wisely but too well." For the murder of her newborn babe Effie has been condemned to die. Only the queen can help to save her now. Jeanie pleads:

Oh, madam, if ever ye kend what it was to suffer for and with a sinning and suffering creature, sae tossed that she can neither be ca'd fit to live or die, have some compassion on our misery! Save an honest house from disaster, and an unhappy girl, not yet eighteen years of age, from an early and awful death! Alas, it is not when we sleep soft and wake merrily ourselves that we think on other people's sufferings. Our hearts are waxed light within us then, and we are for righting our ain wrongs and fighting our ain battles. But when the hour of trouble comes to the mind or the body—and seldom may it visit your Leddyship—and when the hour of death comes, that comes to high and low—lang and late may it be yours!—Oh, my Leddy, then it isna what we hae dune for oursells, but what we hae dune for others, that we think on maist pleasantly.

Erelong Effie Deans was set free. To what can we attribute the spell that her older sister cast over the heart of cold Queen Caroline? To naught save the impact of character and the charm of personality. For a much more recent object lesson, this one from real life, turn to Alice Freeman Palmer.[3] Needless to tell, she differed from Jeanie Deans as much as the latter was unlike

Abigail. No one of the three could have occupied the place that the God of all wisdom planned for either of the others. Even so, all three must have been alike in charm. That in turn grew out of religion. What is your home church doing to rear such girls and women for the world of tomorrow?

4. *How God blesses the beautiful peacemaker* (vv. 32-42). For sheer romance this tale vies with the Book of Esther. To begin with, Abigail averted the shedding of blood. Throughout the centuries we men have failed to prevent one war after another. Perhaps we should rely more largely on the tact and the charm of such good women as Madame Chiang Kai-shek. If we had such diplomats at the peace table, we might be sure that the sessions would open with prayer. We could even hope for peace on earth, good will among men—all to be ushered in through the sweet reasonableness of Christian women with charm.

Once again, our lovely peacemaker Abigail won for herself a worthy husband and a happy home. All this makes us think about Ruth. Some of us believe that a good woman comes into the fullness of her powers when she lives and shines at the heart of a family circle. There she can wield her magic spell day after day, secure in the favor of God and men. There she can gently guide her sons and daughters into paths of honor and peace.

In view of such an ideal let us look at the facts today. From the standpoint of morals we may not object to much that we see and hear on the streets and in places of amusement. Still we feel confident that a woman or a girl can exert more influence over men and boys by being sweetly feminine than by acting like a man. Hence we ought to be asking: What is our home church doing to rear girls and young women with character and charm? How else can we hope to contribute our rightful share to the rebuilding of a war-blasted world?

[3] See *The Life of Alice Freeman Palmer*, by her husband, George Herbert Palmer, Houghton, Mifflin, 1908.

CHAPTER 21

THE TRICKERY OF A SPIRITUALIST

I Samuel 28

ONCE MORE WE NOTE THE WRITER'S SKILL IN THE USE OF CONTRASTING colors. We have been thinking about a good woman's charms. Now we are to study his account of a bad woman's wiles. Thus we enter the field once known as spiritualism and now called spiritism. We shall find the subject bristling with difficulties. Indeed, we shall raise more questions than we can answer. Throughout we shall assume that a few mediums have been sincere and high-minded. However, we shall fix our attention on one of many deliberate deceivers. Whether or not a particular medium has been deluded, who can say? But we feel sure that countless fortunetellers and soothsayers have been guilty of willful fraud. Now we turn to our specific case.

1. *The time when spiritism flourishes* (vv. 1-7). Such practices abound in the wake of a devastating war. In Israel the tides of battle had been running against the so-called children of God. More than a few of them had resorted to "witches" who professed to be in touch with the unseen world. In our own country spiritism seems to have arisen during the years that led up to the War Between the States. Because of that bloody conflict the new movement grew apace, especially in cities along the Atlantic Seaboard. After World War I still larger throngs of grief-stricken parents frequented seances in quest of word from the other world. In the wake of World War II, especially in lands that have been left with money, fraudulent mediums are reaping a harvest.

Spiritism flourishes most among defeated folk. For example,

think of Central Europe. If those bewildered people can scrape together the needed cash, they will flock to all sorts of soothsayers. As for those who have no such resources, they must look elsewhere. Even when childlike people have lost their houses and their all, the typical fortuneteller refuses to intercede with the unseen spirits unless the suppliants can pay in advance. In fact, thirst for pelf often distinguishes the imposter from the high-minded medium. However she may be deluded, a sincere seeker after truth would never turn away a penniless suppliant.

As for the person who consults the "familiar spirit," his distress may spring from causes within. King Saul, for instance, had previously gone through battle after battle without any such commerce with the unseen world. But at last his inner reserves began to fail. He felt sure that he faced certain defeat and shame. His active imagination, all distraught, must have conjured up enemies worse by far than the mightiest warriors in the flesh. In terms of our day he could have sung:

> My foes are ever near me,
> Around me and within.

He knew all about

> the storms of passion,
> The murmurs of self-will.

But through lack of religion he could not have prayed:

> O speak to reassure me,
>
> . . . .
>
> Thou Guardian of my soul.

Nor could he have sung:

> Draw thou nearer,
> And shield my soul from sin.[1]

[1] Excerpts from the familiar hymn "O Jesus, I Have Promised," a confirmation song by John E. Bode, 1868.

161

This man's distress sprang from lack of religion as well as from psychological maladjustment. If the king had lived in right relation with God, he would have felt no irresistible impulse to consult the witch of Endor. During his earlier years as king, Saul had been able to depend on Samuel as a spiritual counselor. As long as the king could go to that dear old friend and "pastor," he felt no need of other contacts with the spiritual world. He could solve each problem as it arose. But when the man of God departed, the king was at his wit's end. Having nowhere else to turn, he decided to consult a necromancer, although in earlier years he had done his utmost to drive such wizards out of the land.[2] But in his hour of despair he stooped to the folly from which he had striven to shield his people. What a miserable spectacle for a mighty warrior who had once received the Spirit of God!

In those closing years of his tragic career King Saul discovered that he could not pray. Doubtless he had been reared in the home of a praying mother. In early manhood he had relied on the intercessions of Samuel. But in the hour of crisis, when the king most needed to ascertain the will of God, he found the heavens as brass. Instead of being filled with the power of the Holy Spirit, the poor fellow felt God-forsaken.

Much the same inner causes have contributed to the growth of spiritism in our own times. Before World War II millions of earth's children tried to get along without God. Now that sorrow has struck home to their hearts, they know not how to use "the outward and ordinary means of grace." If they could be sure of guidance from above, they might not resort to "familiar spirits." But when bewildered mortals have no pastor who stands ready to intercede, and no church to offer a friendly shelter, they reach out for what spiritism offers. In every city parish, and in many an open countryside, future devotees of spiritism live all about the officers and members of the local church.

[2] I Sam. 28:3b. Cf. Lev. 19:31; Deut. 18:10; I Sam. 15:23.

Where does spiritism find its most ardent followers? Chiefly among former adherents of Protestant bodies. During the past hundred years this movement has grown largely through the accession of those who have dropped out of evangelical churches. When burdened men and women fail to find in the local sanctuary and the counsels of its minister the serenity and the uplift that our religion stands ready to provide, they cease to attend church. Then we list them under "losses by removal," and we look about for others to fill the vacant places. Some day "when life tumbles in," these unchurched folk will turn elsewhere for heart's ease. Unfortunately, many of them will hie away to subterranean channels.

2. *The way spiritism often works* (vv. 8-14). This necessarily brief treatment of this subject makes the facts seem too simple. Surely we can find no fault with such psychical research as that of Professor Joseph B. Rhine and his associate scientists at Duke University. If those high-minded searchers after truth discover anything of lasting worth, we shall rejoice. Still we have no reason to believe that the witch of Endor could have qualified for membership in a Society for Psychical Research.

The more sordid kinds of spiritism lend themselves to gross deception. A typical seance takes place at night. In the case of Saul the interview called for a disguise. With many of the devotees today there may be no desire to do wrong. Even so, a movement that prefers darkness rather than light plays into the hands of designing men. For example, think of the Ku Klux Klan as revived and revamped after World War I. For a while the reconditioned Klan threatened to capture the majority of the votes in farming states of the Middle West. The movement enlisted hosts of sincere men, including ministers, who never dreamed of breaking our country's laws. But when they donned white robes and went out to hold secret conclaves by night they could not deter base men from employing the same tactics in order to do wrong. This one element of disguise and stealth should be enough to keep any thoughtful person from resorting to the haunts of darkness.

The devil always prefers to do his deeds of darkness at night. The witch of Endor strove to bring up a spirit from below. Where did she suppose that the man of God made his home in the unseen world? Down among the things of earth, or up in the realms of glory? Of course these matters of time and space have little to do with the realities of the unseen world. In that mystic realm there can be no question of up or down, for God dwells everywhere. Nevertheless, in our noblest hours we gaze up into heaven, and in our blackest moments we peer down on the earth. God seems to have made us so. At least He never intended that one of His children should slink away to a law-breaking fortune-teller and then give her money to look down for the spirit of a saint who dwells beyond "the light of setting suns."

The wrong kind of spiritism also relies on vagueness. What did that fortuneteller profess to have seen? Nothing more than an old man covered with a robe. If she had had any cunning at all, she must have known that the king would expect to hear about an elderly seer clad in a mantle. Saul himself appears to have seen nothing. He had to depend on the word of a law-breaking woman who had no reason for telling him the truth. From that hour to this, when has the habitué of such a cave ever beheld anything worth seeing? When has he ever heard anything worth repeating?

Three thousand years have gone by since the king went to call on the witch of Endor. In all that time what has spiritism contributed to our knowledge of God and the unseen world? For light about Him and the way everlasting we still must turn to the Scriptures in the spirit of prayer. "The secret things belong unto the Lord our God; but the things that are revealed belong unto us and to our children for ever, that we may do all the

words of this law." [3] Why then do we insist on learning what our
Heavenly Father does not wish us to know, at least not now?
Never shall we enter into those mysteries until we take up our
abode in the house not made with hands. "Now we see in a
mirror, darkly; but then face to face." [4]

Here someone may ask: "Why must we think of this woman as
an imposter? May she not have been self-deceived?" Perhaps so,
for the biblical record seems far from clear to us now. No interpretation satisfies every student of the Book.[5] The present way of
regarding the facts encounters at least one obstacle: the sacred
writer says that the woman actually beheld the form of the
deceased prophet, and that the king really heard the voice of his
well-known friend. In each statement the Hebrew author appears
to be recounting everything from the standpoint of King Saul
and his two male escorts. In much the same fashion the writer
could have said that the sun arose the next morning. From his
point of view that appeared to take place. In like manner the
king thought that the woman had seen the dead seer, and that
Saul had heard the voice of Samuel.

"How could the king have been mistaken about the voice of
his beloved friend?" someone may ask. Surreptitiously the woman
may have resorted to ventriloquism. An adept in that art could
have impersonated the dead prophet. In the Greek version of our
chapter the term "familiar spirit" is translated to mean a ventriloquist. Literally, the Greek word means "prophesying from the
belly." According to a standard book in its field, the term was
"used mostly of women who delivered oracles by this means" [6]
—that is, by the use of ventriloquism.

[3] Deut. 29:29.
[4] I Cor. 13:12a.
[5] For other interpretations see *The International Critical Commentary* and *The
Cambridge Bible*.
[6] H. G. Liddell and Robert Scott, *A Greek-English Lexicon* (American Book,
1882), p. 467.

According to this interpretation the fortuneteller could easily have deceived a man like Saul. By resorting to ventriloquism, which must have been her chief stock in trade, she could make him think that he was listening to his departed friend. As for what the deceased prophet is supposed to have said, any ventriloquist bright enough to set up in business as a medium could have figured out everything that this one told the distraught king. Such a way of looking at the facts surely accords with what we know about spiritism. With certain exceptions here and there, the mediums have been deceivers and the devoteees have been dupes.

A practical example of the ventriloquist's wiles comes from over the sea.

Louis Brabant, *valet de chambre* of Francis I, is said to have fallen in love with a beautiful and rich heiress in Paris. He was rejected by the parents as a low, unsuitable match. However, the father dying, he visited the widow, and on his first appearance in the house she heard herself accosted in a voice resembling that of her dead husband, which seemed to proceed from above:

"Give my daughter to Louis Brabant, who is a man of great fortune and excellent character. I now endure the inexpressible torments of purgatory for having refused her to him. Obey this injunction and I shall soon be delivered. You will provide a worthy husband for your daughter and procure everlasting repose for the soul of your poor husband."

The dread summons—which had no appearance of proceeding from Louis, whose countenance exhibited no change, and whose lips were motionless—was instantly complied with.[7]

In much the same fashion the ventriloquist secured enough wealth to carry out his part of the contract. He went to call on a rich banker in Lyons, who had been guilty of usury and

[7] Robert E. Sherwood, *Here We Are Again; Recollections of an Old Circus Clown* (Bobbs-Merrill, 1926), pp. 141-43.

extortion. Impersonating the banker's father, who had gone to purgatory, the voice told the son to give Louis Brabant ten thousand crowns for the ransom of Christians suffering as slaves under the Turks. Thus the banker son would atone for his misdeeds, and likewise extricate his father from the torments of purgatory. For both father and son the only alternative would be the fires of hell. After a second message of the sort, the banker gave the ventriloquist the amount he demanded. Then the young scoundrel, suddenly become affluent, married the beautiful heiress. Doubtless the two lived unhappily ever after.

We have no way of verifying the tale. Surely it sounds fantastic enough to be true. But it seems that the following account can be accepted at face value. It has to do with such high-minded and honorable believers in psychical research as Sir Oliver Lodge and Sir Arthur Conan Doyle. To his dying hour each of those gentlemen stood out as a public exponent of spiritism. In 1931, a year after the death of "Sherlock Holmes," the daily press of our land reported the confession of his favorite medium, Nino Pecararo. For more than eleven years he had hoodwinked Sir Arthur Conan Doyle, as well as a host of other seekers after a word from the beyond.[8]

This famous medium acknowledged that he had never seen or heard a spirit and that he did not think anyone else had ever done so. He averred that he had grown weary of giving seances and then letting spiritism reap the rewards from his trickery. He would have understood why the brilliant magician Harry Houdini scoffed at the pretensions of spiritualistic mediums. Publicly for years Houdini offered to duplicate by mechanical means any feat that such a medium could perform. Up until the hour of his untimely death in 1926 he never once had to carry out his part of the contract. In that year the people of New York City are said to have paid spiritualistic mediums five

[8] For a newspaper report see *The Christian Observer*, Louisville, May 20, 1931.

million dollars. Today the "rake-off" must be vastly more. "Wherefore do ye spend money for that which is not bread? and your labor for that which satisfieth not? hearken diligently unto me." [9] Thus saith the Lord.

3. *The tragedy of spiritism* (vv. 15-19). At least in the case of King Saul, this sort of folly appealed to the Godforsaken: "God is departed from me, and answereth me no more!" The poor man might rather have said: "I have forsaken the God of my fathers, and I know not how to pray." Here we have a concrete instance of unanswered prayer. Ofttimes we speak of prayer as being unanswered when really it has been answered with God's "No." For example, the Lord denied the petition of the Apostle Paul for the removal of his "stake in the flesh." [10] With neither Saul nor Paul did our God fail to answer. The one man had not prayed; the other received his reply.

Unable to get in touch with the "Unknown God," King Saul sought out a fortuneteller. That visit marked the beginning of his end. If he had not gone to see that witch, he might have met his death the next day. Even so, the leader of God's hosts ought not to have spent his last night on earth down in a murky cave with a woman who was defying the laws of God and men. What a sorry way to prepare for the battle on the morrow, and for the life beyond this earth!

Now let us glance at the carnage on the ensuing day. There we see how King Saul lost his sons, laid down his life, and thus forfeited the kingdom. We learn how a man's follies as he draws near to death may neutralize all his earlier achievements. However, if we regard this friend as the victim of mental disorders we shall not hold him morally responsible for his misdeeds. In the Scriptures we never see him held up like Absalom or Judas as an example of unspeakable infamy. Rather do we learn to look

[9] Isa. 55:2.
[10] II Cor. 12:1-9.

on King Saul with pity. Hence we should resolve not to let our own impulses drive us on such a tragic fate.

What then shall we conclude about spiritism? Even at best we find in it nothing needful for the children of God. If we would come close to Him, why resort to some murky cave instead of to the house of prayer? Do we not believe that God is waiting to give heed, and that He answers the call of faith? When have we ever known Him to ignore any sinner or saint who really prayed? "An upright man can do a great deal by prayer when he tries." [11]

From another point of view our hearts go out to the devotees of spiritism. In the home church we have failed to provide what they need. At least we have not made them aware that they could find solace at the sanctuary and through the "pastor's hour." [12] Now we know that almost every household needs the consolations of the gospel. What provision are we making to bring these disconsolate friends the peace of God and the hope of life eternal?

For an ideal turn to the sacred art of Florence or Venice. Note how Raphael or one of his pupils sets forth the Madonna and her Babe. Near the top of the canvas the artist shows a glimpse of the sky. Should it not be so whenever war-weary friends come to the house of the Lord? At times the message of the hour relates to the life beyond. When the sermon has to do with things here and now, the hymns and the prayers may include a vista of the unseen and eternal. Thus we may help every friend in the pew to behold the "rainbow round about the throne."

At least once a year there can be a few sermons about what lies beyond the grave. Such messages often come most fitly at night, or at vespers. Instead of throwing stones at spiritism and

---

[11] Jas. 5:16*b* (Goodspeed).

[12] See Blackwood, "The Value of a Pastor's Hour," chap. xxiv of *Pastoral Work*, Westminster, 1945.

other movements for people who mourn, why not lead these friends to behold the glory that streams from many a page in the New Testament? Do we not know, as William Sanday used to say at Oxford, that in the New Testament the center of gravity lies beyond the grave? If so, why should we not lead our grief-stricken friends to look on death and the hereafter in the radiance that streams from the Great White Throne?

Every parish needs a personal counselor such as Samuel. Our chaplain sons who have come home from across the seas have learned how to deal, one by one, with strong men in distress. Those stalwart clergymen also need to excel in comforting women. The vast majority of pastors here at home seem determined to master this fine art. Why should not every ministering servant of God learn from Samuel how to be a good shepherd of souls? When every local church has the right sort of pastor, the members will never stray off into the forbidden walks of spiritism.

CHAPTER 22

THE SHAMEFULNESS OF SELF-MURDER

I Samuel 31

AGAIN WE TACKLE A DIFFICULT PROBLEM. AMONG OTHER ADVANTAGES, the plan of working our way through a book of the Bible leads us to subjects that we might otherwise evade. In the pulpit the wise minister deals with suicide only indirectly. Otherwise he might help to plant the idea in minds not completely balanced. Even so, every pastor needs to think of self-murder with reference to World War II and the ensuing days of "peace." He should be aware that suicide was widely advertized during the war, and still more widely after the collapse of Germany and Japan. Who knows how many of our own strong men and women are now being tempted to self-murder?

At present we are to deal with the matter biblically. In the record about King Saul at Gilboa we find the materials for a case study of suicide. Such a tragedy seldom emerges in the Scriptures. The ancient Hebrews rarely resorted to self-murder. They thought so highly of the human body that they hesitated to destroy this handiwork of God. Nevertheless, the Bible affords a few examples: King Saul, Ahithophel, Zimri, and Judas.[1] If these cases are typical they show that self-murder takes place most often among strong men who have suffered a reversal of fortune. At any rate Saul had once been a hero of renown. "How are the mighty fallen!"

1. *The conditions that drive a strong man to suicide* (vv. 1-8). In the days of King Saul widespread irreligion had carried over

[1] See I Sam. 31:4; II Sam. 17:23; I Kings 16:18; Matt. 27:5.

171

from the time of the Judges. Even the ruler had lost his early contacts with God. Saul had striven in vain to extricate himself from the consequences of his rashness and folly. At last he was forced to face military reverses and resulting shame. He found that load too much for his war-weary nerves. In the battle at Gilboa he had to witness a crushing defeat. While he saw his troops in flight he learned that he had lost his three sons, including Jonathan. The distraught father knew that he himself would soon be taken captive. He could hope for no mercy at the hands of those bloodthirsty Philistines.

In such an hour who would not consider the matter of self-murder? More than a thousand years after, a Jewish historian recounts an experience somewhat parallel. In his *Wars of the Jews* Josephus tells of his capture by the Romans and of his debating with himself the wisdom of suicide. He concludes that self-murder would be unworthy of a strong man, as well as an affront to God. The stress falls on lack of courage: "He is equally a coward who will not die when he is obliged to die, and he who will die when he is not obliged to do so. . . . I should esteem that pilot an arrant coward, who, out of fear of a storm, should sink the ship of his own accord."[2]

King Saul had become that kind of coward. Even when he faced certain defeat and ensuing shame, why did he not think of others? Why did he not rally and hearten his troops? Instead of forgetting self in action, he pleaded with his armor-bearer: "Draw thy sword, and thrust me through." When that fearful attendant refused to lay hands on the Lord's anointed, Saul killed himself. Thus he escaped the indignities the Philistines would have heaped upon such a living captive. For a similar case, wholly hypothetical, imagine what certain troopers would have done if they could have captured Adolf Hitler. At the present writing it seems that he averted such a fate by resorting to self-murder.

[2] *Works*, tr. William Whiston (Philadelphia, 1857), II, 270-71.

Thus we come directly to the question "Is suicide ever justifiable? Is it ever the easy way out?" Easy for whom? Out into what? Instead of discussing the matter theoretically, let us consider a recent case. Why did Pastor Martin Niemöller in his German prison camp give his word of honor that he would not do away with himself? He had considered the question with care. He concluded that suicide would indicate distrust of God, disregard for loved ones, and disdain of self. Are not these the tests that show the rightness or the wrongness of any deed? How does it affect one's relations with God, with others, and with self? In short, with Immanuel Kant, so live that if everyone else did so this would be an ideal world.

For a religious view of the matter turn to *Pilgrim's Progress*. Unfortunately, the passage does not usually appear in modern editions. Bunyan's narrative relates to Doubting Castle, under the thralldom of Giant Despair. The record concerns the sort of despondency that leads to self-murder. Christian is speaking: "The life that we now live is miserable; for my part I know not whether it is better to live thus or die out of hand. . . . The grave is more easy than this dungeon. Shall we be ruled by the giant?" [8]

In reply Hopeful brings forth ten arguments against self-murder. Some of them follow here word for word; others appear only in substance. (1) "The Lord of the country to which we are going hath said, 'Thou shalt do no murder.' . . . Much more then are we forbidden to take the giant's counsel to kill ourselves." (2) "He that kills another can but commit murder upon his body, but for one to kill himself is to kill both body and soul at once." (3) "Thou talkest of ease in the grave, but hast thou forgotten the hell whither for certain the murderers go?" (4) Others have escaped from the clutches of Giant Despair. (5) God may cause him to die, or at least to grow careless. (6) By watch-

[8] *The Complete Works of John Bunyan*, ed. J. P. Gulliver (Philadelphia, 1853), pp. 145-46.

fulness thou canst escape. (7) Think of thy former deliverances from such foes. (8) Remember that Hopeful is with thee in the dungeon. (9) Summon to thine aid the Christian virtue of Patience. (10) Avoid the shame that becometh not a believer in Christ.

The allegory reaches a climax in the account of Christian's escape. Just before the dawning of the day, after a night spent in prayer, he exclaims: "I have a key in my bosom called Promise, that will, I am persuaded, open any lock in Doubting Castle." So it proved. Soon the pilgrims found themselves free. Then they began to contrive means of preventing others from falling into the clutches of Giant Despair. The recent captives set up a pillar on which they wrote: "Over this stile is the way to Doubting Castle, which is kept by Giant Despair, who despiseth the King of the Celestial Country, and seeks to destroy the holy pilgrims." Many therefore that followed after read what was written and escaped from peril. Why should any man in his senses commit self-murder?

2. *The barbarous customs of war* (vv. 7-10). Victory in battle may unleash the most diabolical passions. King Saul had made no mistake in dreading the ferocity of those triumphant tigers. After he had killed himself they cut off his head, and then they fastened his torso on the city wall. What they planned to do with that head, who can tell? All of this would seem doubly dreadful to the Hebrews. They looked on the body as a gift from above, and on the king's body as that of one anointed by God. They could see that even by suicide poor Saul had not escaped the worst of indignities. As with most cases of self-murder, he left others to endure the anguish of defeat and shame.

Thus far we have thought little about the effect on others. Apart from the affront to God, and the weakness in self, what of the loved ones who survived? Would the Hebrew people wish to remember that their first king had killed himself? Would the family circle wish to recall that its most distinguished son had committed suicide? Except with one who has become insane, there can be no solace for friends and loved ones who must live on amid the ashes of dead hopes. As for the victim himself, suicide leads out into midnight darkness and despair.

3. *The contrasting trait of loyalty* (vv. 11-13). Once again our author lets the light shine in to relieve the gloom. Now he introduces the men of Gilead, whom Saul had befriended.[4] After the death of the king and his sons, those men from beyond the Jordan imperiled their lives in order to rescue the mutilated bodies and accord them honorable burial. Thus those people from Gilead expressed their gratitude, even toward the dead. In days of war such loyalty and kindness help to relieve the feeling of futility and despair.

Kindness stands out as "the highest human excellence." Thus spoke a master preacher of yesterday, George A. Gordon, of Boston. In a noteworthy sermon he declared that kindness indicates "a sense of the greatness and the pathos of human life." He said that classic dramas serve as "windows through which the student looks out upon the tragic world. The world itself is beyond—wide-reaching, mysterious, terrible with woe. . . . The kind man cannot look upon this vast scene of error and pain without pity. His heart is moved with compassion." Meantime, in days after a war, "Satan, in the form of unkindness, is still walking to and fro in the earth, unbelieving, cynical, frivolous, heartless, relentless, and armed with power to afflict and curse mankind."[5]

In its upper reaches kindness means religion at work. "Religion is the loving kindness and tender mercy of God revealed to the world in the teaching, ministry, and death of Jesus Christ. . . . We have a God whose highest attribute is not justice, but kind-

[4] See I Sam. 11:1-13.
[5] *Through Man to God* (Houghton, Mifflin, 1906), pp. 199-214.

175

ness, not supreme regard for law, but supreme concern for man."[6]

The facts about the kind burial of the king might lead to a study of the body. That seems to have been the best thing about Saul. Unlike other rulers in the East, he kept that body pure. Hence Andrew Bruce Davidson has written about the king's "immaculate moral life, so singular in an Oriental monarch, and in such contrast even with his successor." How then should a man of God look on his body?

The Bible teaches one to regard it as the gift of Heaven. Among all of God's handiwork, what can compare with the human body? "Know ye not that your body is a temple of the Holy Spirit?"[7] Does any other thing on earth have the assurance of sharing in the final resurrection and the life everlasting? No one understands what he often says in church: "I believe in . . . the resurrection of the body." Even so, everyone should rejoice in what those words suggest about the future glory of the spiritual body.

Whether it stands or falls, the temple of the Holy Spirit ought to be treated with loving care. In time of war it may become a man's duty to lay down his life. If so, all that remains of him afterward should be dealt with tenderly. For such a conception of the body we may turn to the Book of Ruth. That charming domestic romance comes from the period of the Judges, perhaps a little before the time of King Saul. Listen to the heroine of the simple tale: "Entreat me not to leave thee, and to return from following after thee; for whither thou goest I will go; and where thou lodgest, I will lodge; thy people shall be my people, and thy God my God; where thou diest, will I die, and there will I be buried."[8] What loyalty, even unto death! What a contrast to the selfishness of suicide!

[6] *Ibid.*, p. 214.
[7] I Cor. 6:19.
[8] Ruth 1:16-17*a.*

THE SHAMEFULNESS OF SELF-MURDER

What has all of this to do with the work of the pastor now? Much every way! In a world where suicide has become common, he can uphold the ideals of the Scriptures. In the pulpit and elsewhere he can teach the sanctity of a man's body. In the study the clergyman can deal gently yet firmly with the returned soldier or sailor whom shattered nerves and blasted hopes have driven to the brink of self-murder. Why should not every parish minister face the fact that World War II has increased every man's difficulty in living according to the ethical standards of Holy Writ? In short, my brother, make ready now to deal with that next case of contemplated suicide.

CHAPTER 23

THE CAUSES OF A LEADER'S COLLAPSE

THE TIME HAS COME FOR A BIRD'S-EYE VIEW OF SAUL'S CAREER. The task will not prove easy. Who can survey that life as a whole and size it up with precision? One observer may wax eulogistic,[1] whereas another seems severe. The truth lies between the two extremes. The first king of Israel could qualify neither as a genius nor as a demon, neither as a beatific saint nor as a hopeless sinner. His life and work stand out best of all in the eulogy pronounced by his successor: "How are the mighty fallen!" [2]

These words make one think of a massive oak, or of a Roman temple. If it be a temple, see it lying in ruins. One can almost behold a Roman shrine, worthy of note for size, and not a Greek work of art, famous for classic beauty. As an example take one of those stupendous Roman temples that lie in ruins at Baalbek. What a way of regarding a former king as we bid him farewell! We behold him "unwept, unhonored, and unsung," except by David. We ask, "What has caused King Saul's collapse?" For a tentative answer we now look back.

1. *The most promising man in the nation.* When Young Saul became king he bade fair to become the mightiest leader in Old Testament history. From our human and outward point of view he appeared to have everything heart could desire in a ruler of men. For example, we must admire his physique. Our minds turn to Adam Bede in George Eliot's moving tale, or to Alois Lang

[1] See Pfeiffer, *op. cit.,* p. 359.
[2] II Sam. 1:25, 27.

178

at the Passion Play in Oberammergau. We behold the first Hebrew monarch towering above other men as the Matterhorn rises above the surrounding Alps. "Take him for all in all, I shall not look upon his like again."

As a more recent specimen of robust physical manhood think of Phillips Brooks. What a body the Lord gave that lover of men! Whenever he walked through the slums of East Boston his presence made childlike people feel that the Lord Jesus had passed by, and that He had smiled on their little ones playing in the streets. Of such a personage Isaiah wrote: "A man shall be as a hiding-place from the wind, and a covert from the tempest, as streams of water in a dry place, as the shade of a great rock in a weary land." [3]

Like the beloved pastor in Boston, the first king of Israel received from the Lord a winsome personality. What that means, who can know? Personality shows itself in the ability to lead men who otherwise might wander as sheep without a shepherd. In young Saul personality signified a blending of manliness and modesty with courage and caution. Then too he possessed the indefinable something that makes everybody love a man despite all his failings. As long as the two of them lived, King Saul filled a large place in the heart of Samuel. So did the ruler win the affection of young David. In fact, despite all his aberrations, Saul appears to have made no personal enemies.

Then too his reign led to achievements worthy of note. Think of the difference between the partial anarchy when he commenced to rule and the comparative orderliness when he laid down his arms. Remember that he became the national leader during the chaotic days of the Judges. Note the many social advances before he gave way to King David. For all those marks of progress reserve much of the credit for the prophet Samuel. But remember that they occurred during the reign of King

[3] Isa. 32:2.

Saul. In his lifetime the people began to emerge from semibarbarism and to make ready for their ultimate contributions to the Kingdom of God.

If Saul had done nothing more than hold the people together, that would have entitled him to a place in the sun. Before his time, as well as afterward, they tended to split in two and form separate groups, much as our own land threatened to become known as the South and the North. During Saul's lifetime he prevented those two divergent sections from falling asunder. He must have known that if each half went off by itself both parts might be swallowed up by hostile powers.

In various other ways the kingship of Saul witnessed advances. Notwithstanding all of that, he never fulfilled the promise of his youth. According to Phillips Brooks, the morning of Saul's life dawned as bright as a Boston day in June, whereas the evening of his career became as dismal as a New England day in December.[4] Unlike Saul of Tarsus, who began ignobly and ended gloriously, King Saul started his career with the favor of God, and men but finished it in shame and disgrace. He might have served Robert Browning as an object lesson for that poem "The Lost Leader." Strange to tell, both Saul the king and Paul the apostle belonged to the little tribe of Benjamin.

2. *The debacle of Saul's latter days.* Little by little, then more and more, the king lost his hold on the Lord. In fact, he seems never to have known the Almighty as his personal God.[5] As long as he could rely on the counsels of Samuel, the ruler led his people admirably. But as soon as he tried to stand alone, he failed. No doubt such a way of regarding the facts makes them appear too simple. Even so, the following summary makes clear why many a strong man fails.

[4] See his study of King Saul, "The Choice Young Man," *Sermons* (Dutton, 1910), V, 89-105.
[5] For this point of view see A. B. Davidson, "Saul's Reprobation," a masterly study in *The Called of God* (T. & T. Clark, Edinburgh, 1903), pp. 141-61.

THE CAUSES OF A LEADER'S COLLAPSE

King Saul began trying to do God's will in His way and with His power. Hence he prospered in every good work, but only for a season. Then he tried to carry out God's will in Saul's way and with Saul's strength, which proved to be weakness. Thus he brought on an endless chain of disappointments and reverses. Before long the poor fellow was not even attempting to do the will of God. Soon he collapsed. Has it not been so with many a strong leader? For instance, look at Cardinal Wolsey in the court of Henry VIII. Stripped of all his honors after he had begun to grow old, charged with disloyalty to the monarch whom he had blindly obeyed, the Cardinal exclaimed: "If I had served my God as diligently as I have done my king, He would not have given me over in my gray hairs!"[6]

Saul owed his collapse to "religious incapacity." So declares A. B. Davidson.

[The king] had not the faculty of knowing what religion meant. He might know that religion meant a full surrender of one's will to God; but he was too blunt, in a religious sense, to understand what full surrender was. . . . [He lacked] religious depth, . . . the one quality necessary for success and happiness. He was king in the kingdom of God, but he failed to comprehend the meaning of the kingdom.

He never rose to the full conception of what God's kingdom was, and demanded. He had never thought himself, or felt himself, into it. It had always stood outside of him, as something which he could not realize. He was conscious of this, and he betrayed his consciousness in the way he spoke to Samuel. He felt that Samuel stood to the Lord in different relations than himself. He always speaks to him [Samuel] of "the Lord thy God." His [Saul's] very honesty hinders him from saying "the Lord my God." . . .

Saul was used to teach a great lesson to the Church of God, and to the world: to show what profound qualities the king of God's king-

---

[6] See Samuel R. Gardiner, *A Student's History of England* (Longmans, Green, 1898), p. 384.

dom needs, what consecration to God, what perfect obedience and spirituality. Saul's failure taught this more conspicuously than his success would have done. But he was used as a dead thing, irrespective of his own interests.[7]

So much for the facts in general. Now let us enumerate Saul's major blunders. We shall not refer to them as sins, for we know not how serious was his mental unbalance, his moral irresponsibility. Whatever the label we attach to his aberrations, his chief shortcomings appear to have numbered six.[8] Each of them in its different fashion constituted a defiance of God's holy will. First of all, the king showed impatience that led to ill-considered action. Again, he displayed rashness that might have caused the slaying of his son Jonathan. Once more, Saul disobeyed God, because "he did not know what obedience meant." Still further, he yielded to envy, which led to the attempted murder of his most devoted liegeman. In addition, the king manifested disloyalty to the laws of God by consulting a fortuneteller. Last of all, he committed the irrevocable deed of self-murder. What a catalogue of shortcomings in the career of a king!

Because he had lost his hold on God, Saul gradually forfeited his control over himself and over his people. He was forced to witness their turning away from him as leader and their growing enthusiasm for David as hero. In Saul's lucid hours he must have sensed that he alone was to blame for that falling away. He must have foreseen that he could never occupy a place among the immortals in the Hebrew Hall of Fame, but that he would go down in history as a tragic failure. "Unstable as water, thou shalt not excel." [9]

Worst of all, the king seems to have grieved the Holy Spirit. What that means in detail, who can say? However, a few facts

---

[7] *Op. cit.,* pp. 144-57.
[8] See I Sam. 13–15, 17, 28, 31.
[9] Gen. 49:4*a* (A.V.).

182

emerge. At the beginning of his public career the young leader is said to have received the Spirit. That must have signified the power of God in the life of His servant. Such an enduement expresses itself in practical guidance, with abundance of strength to do the will of God. The Holy Spirit likewise imparts the poise that men expect in their leader. The power of God in the heart of a ruler makes him strong, wise, and humble.

When the Holy Spirit departs from a soul where He has dwelt for a time, darkness and despair ensue. To be empowered by the Lord, to be guided by Him, and to be used for His glory, but at last to be laid aside as worse than useless—what a reversal of fortune! To have the strength of a rock, and to become like shifting sand; to seem as mighty as a river within its banks, and then to become as weak as water spilled on the ground—what a tragic anticlimax! In still other terms, the massive temple now lies in ruins. "How are the mighty fallen!"

Let the parting word come from A. B. Davidson:

It is not for us to censure, but to pity. Subsequent Scripture has no word of censure for Saul. It says only that God took away His mercy from him, that he should be no more king—nothing more. He was the first king of God's kingdom; and we desire to think that, having such a place, he was not cast away.

We leave his faults where we leave our own—at the feet of the true King of the kingdom of God, who did not leave the kingdom a ruin, as Saul did, but who established it with judgment and with justice, from henceforth even for ever; and who is the propitiation for our sins; and not for ours only, but for the sins of the whole world.[10]

[10] *Op. cit.,* p. 161.

Part Three

THE MAN WHO LEADS IN REBUILDING

SECOND SAMUEL, CHAPTERS 1-24

CHAPTER 24

THE SPIRIT OF RECONSTRUCTION

II Samuel 1–3

IN RECENT YEARS ALMOST EVERY NATION ON EARTH HAS DEALT WITH problems of reconstruction after war. Even the countries of South America and of Africa have suffered indirectly. Through the past century more than one power in Europe has faced such issues again and again. How then can we remove from our midst the aftermath of global war? How can we handle the worst of all the debris, that in human bodies and souls? In a sense we must leave to God the remaking of men, one by one. But still we hear Him calling for helpers. How can we qualify? For light on the work of a master rebuilder look at the records about David.

1. *The wise leader's attitude toward the past* (II Sam. 1). The opening chapter of Second Samuel makes clear the prudent attitude toward one's predecessor. The new leader did everything in his power to show respect for the memory of the dead ruler and for the past regime. A smaller man than David might have exulted in the overthrow of the former dynasty. To have done so would have alienated the men on whom the new leader had to rely for the success of the incoming administration. Surely David showed wisdom when he praised all that had proved worthy in the immediate past. That meant speaking well of King Saul, together with Prince Jonathan.

All the while the new leader kept looking forward. Thus he encouraged the people to forget the failures, the heartaches, and the bitterness of the days bygone. He would have them carry into the unknown morrow only the recollection of the true, the

187

beautiful, and the good. This principle applies almost everywhere in our religion. Hence F. W. Robertson has left us a striking sermon about "Christian Progress by Oblivion of the Past." He says in part: "Life, like war, is a series of mistakes, and he is not the best Christian nor the best general who makes the fewest false steps. . . . He is the best who wins the most splendid victories by the retrieval of past mistakes. Forget mistakes; organize victory out of mistakes."[1]

The experience of David shows the wisdom of the forward look. Forget the shortcomings and the blunders, the tragedies and the sins, of days now gone. Carry into the morrow only the memory of forgiven transgressions and the determination to avoid such pitfalls in the future. That would have been Abraham Lincoln's way of reconciling the seceding states after our tragic war. According to James Bryce in his monumental work, *The American Commonwealth,* "There never was a civil war . . . followed by so few severities." Perhaps that is true, but why should there have been any at all? Can we not learn from David the practical wisdom of making "progress by oblivion of the past"?

2. *The beginning of a better era* (II Sam. 2:1-4*a*). The new regime began with prayer. Before David took the first step, he sought guidance from above. Here again he showed practical wisdom. Since he belonged to the tribe of Judah, he started the new work in the South. But he did not know in what center to launch the new movement. When he prayed for special guidance, he was directed to Hebron. David could see its advantages over Bethlehem, his home town. Not only was Hebron one of the ancestral shrines, dear to the hearts of God's people. That stronghold was likewise easy to defend. As long as Judah stood alone, Hebron would serve as the temporary capital city.

At this time David seems to have been about thirty years of age.

[1] *Sermons Preached at Brighton* (new ed., Harper, n.d.), pp. 57-68.

Surely he displayed unusual wisdom for a man that young. At the very start he could see that the new movement needed a geographical center, to impart "visibility and permanence," as well as to afford a rallying point. During all the time Saul had acted as king he never could see that the government needed a "local habitation and a name." With the provincialism of a small-minded farmer he directed affairs from his rural home. By contrast David stands out as a constructive leader. He has a plan, and he begins at once to go forward. What an auspicious beginning, all because he followed the guidance of the Lord in answer to prayer!

3. *The ability to gain new friends* (II Sam. 2:4b-7). During the first days of the administration the leader welcomed an opportunity to show largeness of heart. He learned that the men of Jabesh-gilead had tenderly cared for the body of Saul. At once David went out of his way to honor those public benefactors. His glowing words of appreciation sounded like an excerpt from the Psalms. The new leader had already discovered the magic power of public address. In this respect, at least, David reminds us of Woodrow Wilson.

The magnanimity of David appears more remarkable when we remember the distance between Hebron and Jabesh-gilead. The temporary capital lay southwest of what we know as Jerusalem, whereas Jabesh-gilead seems to have been east of the Jordan, more than a hundred miles distant from Hebron by air. In those early days men did not journey by airplane or motor car. If David had not been farsighted as well as largehearted, he would never have sent messengers all that distance. How did he know that those remote people would welcome his overtures of friendship? Whatever his reasoning, the new commander did all in his power to win friends for himself and for the government.

4. *The barbarism of the times* (II Sam. 2:8–3:39). This section

189

shows that we are dealing with stern and brutal days. Here and there we may find it hard to trace the course of events. All the time we can see one fact: the forces of King David were engaged in a sort of guerrilla warfare which continued for seven and a half years. He had to rely largely on Joab, and on other lieutenants far from ideal. The opposing side included Abner and others by no means ignoble. The strife between these two men led to Joab's killing Abner, a deed that David immediately repudiated. He had sized up Joab as a bloodthirsty warrior, and Abner as a high-minded opponent. Hence the king uttered this glowing tribute: "Know ye not that there is a prince and a great man fallen this day in Israel?"

By such conciliatory measures the young leader commended himself to the people on the opposing side. He showed that he could plan the tedious work of rebuilding the nation. On more than one field of battle he displayed practical foresight and military prowess. Amid guerrilla warfare he proved that personality counted for more than physical force. Mighty as he was in arms, he preferred to win his way by tact and good will. Doubtless he knew that most men are ruled by their hearts and not by their heads. Thus he gradually won the esteem and the affection of countless people both in the North and in the South.

Wherein lay his secret? Really it sounds quite simple. He himself had a heart. He had received it as a gift from God who is love. Herein lies the secret of leadership among men today. Learn how to lead for Him by loving His people. Have a heart as well as a head. How simple, and how sublime!

CHAPTER 25

THE REUNION OF SOUTH AND NORTH

II Samuel 5

FROM THIS TIME ONWARD DAVID WILL RULE OVER THE REUNITED kingdom. That seems to have been the will of the Lord when He commissioned Samuel to anoint the young shepherd at Bethlehem. But seven and a half years had to elapse between the beginning of his reign at Hebron and the reunion of the South with the North. All the while David must have been formulating plans for that consolidation. He must have known that when the two divergent sections agreed to merge, the real work of reunion would have to commence. How did he lead them into a unity more lasting than they had ever enjoyed? Partly by being careful about his initial steps.

1. *The choice of a king for the reunited land* (vv. 1-5). In the selection of their ruler the initiative seems to have come from the tribes in the North. During the years that followed the death of King Saul they had tried to remain separate. They had striven to carry on his dynasty. Gradually the most optimistic of them must have concluded that they had failed. Their only hope of survival lay in uniting with the forces of King David. Hence the leaders of the tribes in the North asked him to become the ruler of the entire land.

All of these proceedings had to do with religion. The leaders in the North expressed their desire to follow David, as one of their own blood and as one chosen of God. "Thou shalt be shepherd of my people Israel, and thou shalt be prince over Israel." What an auspicious start for a new reign! A man of

191

the people—bone of their bone and flesh of their flesh—chosen as king because he belonged to their God! Underlying these actions must have rested the covenant. That meant God's choice of them as His people and their acceptance of Him as their God. In some such spirit of faith and hope those leaders entered into a "solemn league and covenant" with their new king from the South.

Evidently God has a plan for every nation. He lets His children work it out in ways of their own choosing. When they conform to His holy will they look on their ruler as a shepherd. Well did those mountain folk in the Holy Land know the meaning of the word "shepherd." From their earliest years on the hills they had learned that the shepherd must lead. Now that they had decided to merge the two distinct flocks they looked up to David for strong, constructive leadership. By such leadership they expected him to maintain the peace and rebuild the nation. In such a practical philosophy of government God stands first; the people, second; the ruler, third. He becomes their servant, in the name of his Lord.

The new king responded by proposing a religious ceremony. Unlike King Saul, who had to be prompted by Samuel, David looked to God both for sanction and for guidance. Thus he prepared the way for an awesome spectacle. With the leaders of the reunited land he entered into a formal covenant. Doubtless he gave his pledge of honor to rule wisely in the fear of the Lord. He likewise received their promise to follow him in carrying out the will of God. Praying together, both ruler and people thus made ready for the new adventure of rebuilding their part of God's world.

Such a government used to be known as a theocracy. That means

a conception of political organization in which God is the supreme Ruler, so that political laws must be derived from the divine com-

192

mand and earthly rulers must receive authority from God. A theocracy recognized no such thing as secular government, and consequently no distinction between church and state. The Hebrew prophets insisted on a theocratic ideal, and the history of Israel as interpreted in the Old Testament is the story of divine discipline in order to secure a perfect theocracy.[1]

According to the Old Testament, theocracy went back as far as Moses. Under his leadership, as with Joshua, the power over the State rested in the hands of God. In like manner King David held to the principle of theocracy. So did John Calvin at Geneva, and Oliver Cromwell in England. To the present hour the Scottish Covenanters in the United States demand that our nation become a theocracy. They would have our congress put into the Constitution the name of Christ as King. They would require our citizens to pledge Him undying allegiance. However difficult such a program might prove among our polyglot peoples, the ideal impresses us by its grandeur. What have we to take its place?

In the light of this lofty conception turn again to the covenant proposed by King David and ratified by the representatives of the people. Note especially the three parties concerned: the Lord, the people, and the king. As in a young man's covenant of marriage with a maiden, and as in Prince Jonathan's covenant of friendship with a shepherd youth, so in the National Covenant between David and the people everything depended on the favor of God. To this present hour, despite all the changes on the surface of things national and international, this way of looking on government fills us with holy awe. In our own beloved land, as well as beyond the seas, everything good depends on the blessing of God.

2. *The choice of a capital city for the reunited land* (vv. 8-11).

[1] *A Dictionary of Religion and Ethics,* ed. Shailer Mathews and G. B. Smith (Macmillan, 1921), pp. 445-46.

One of the next steps was to locate a new capital. Hebron could not serve ideally as the rallying point for the twelve tribes of Israel. That city had long been identified with Judah, the tribe that furnished the new king. Why not single out some spot that had never become associated with either South or North? From that point of view what location could prove more nearly ideal than the place afterward known as Jerusalem? Thus far it had remained in alien hands. When the ruler of the reunited people led them in capturing that stronghold, he not only gained a site for the future capital and the projected temple. He also established himself as their God-given leader.

A partial analogy appears in our early history. During the Revolutionary War and shortly thereafter the center of our inchoate government was shifted from place to place. At different stages the rallying point seems to have been Philadephia, Princeton, and New York City. No one of those places appeared sufficiently independent of some colony or newborn state. At last, in 1800, the Government took up its abode on a special site that would not thereafter belong to any one commonwealth. For much the same reason, in 1908 the capital of Australia was moved to Canberra, and in 1920 the capital of Turkey was transferred to Ankara.

The selection of the site for a future Hebrew capital showed real statesmanship, which must have come through the guiding hand of the Lord. Even so, if we look closely at the record we shall find one thing still lacking. The narrative does not mention the Ark. In terms of our day, where is the Church? To that vital need of every country, whether new or old, we shall devote a special study. Every nation must have religion as well as government.

CHAPTER 26

THE NEED FOR A VISIBLE CHURCH

II Samuel 6

LET THE ARK OF THE COVENANT STAND FOR THE CHURCH OF GOD. In the Old Testament the Ark appears about two hundred times, sixty-one of them in the books of Samuel. In a sense the Ark dominates this portion of Holy Scripture. Often the setting had to do with war. Whatever the immediate background, the Ark symbolized the presence of God.[1] In fact, the Ark sometimes became a substitute for the Living God. Just now it concerns us with reference to the reunited kingdom.

The new king could see that the reunited tribes needed more than a covenant of religion and a capital city. He quickly perceived the need of a spiritual center, something historic and concrete, to which God's children could turn whenever they wished to ascertain His holy will. In this respect, as in others, the new ruler differed from his predecessor. King Saul had felt no such need of a central sanctuary. He had let the Ark remain at Kiriath-jearim for years. Sometimes we wonder why the Ark should have been so long neglected. May that not have been due to the lack of heart religion in the ruler?

1. *The ceremony of bringing up the Ark* (vv. 1-5). King David believed in religious ceremonial. A man with imagination and a lover of people, he sensed the need of appealing to the eye. In after years he was to lead in setting up lofty standards for the use of music in public worship. There too he stressed the im-

[1] For an illuminating article see "Samuel," *The New Century Bible,* ed. A. R. S. Kennedy (Oxford, n.d.), pp. 321-26.

195

portance of ceremonial.[2] So when the hour came to establish the Ark at the center of the capital city, he arranged for an elaborate procession.

King David strove to make that event momentous, not merely incidental. Wise men still do that on special occasions. They plan most carefully for the dedication of a sanctuary, or the setting apart of a young man for the ministry. In view of New Testament simplicity, some of our friends do not believe in elaborate rites. Notwithstanding these scruples, no one has discovered in the New Testament any reason for refusing to celebrate the chief events of our corporate religious experience. All of us know that the Gospels and the Epistles leave us free to worship as we desire, provided we do so "decently and in order." Many of us feel that the welfare of our children and young people calls for an occasional dramatizing of our holy faith.

The plans of the king for the celebration deserve special study. They called for the participation of thirty thousand men. In proportion to the number of people in the country, especially in the capital city, that number seems enormous. The program was to consist largely of music, especially with "high-sounding cymbals" and other instruments that made "a joyful noise unto the Lord." For this occasion the king is supposed to have written one of our most uplifting psalms, the twenty-fourth. Whoever the author and whatever the date, that song lends itself admirably to the needs of such a festal celebration. Not even the Book of Common Prayer contains any more majestic ceremonial. What antiphonal singing! What versicles and responses! What joy in the public worship of God!

Let us reconstruct the scene as it would concern the use of this psalm. While the vast procession wends its way up the slope toward the eastern gate of the city, the chorus choir leads

<hr>

[2] See Blackwood, *The Fine Art of Public Worship* (Abingdon-Cokesbury, 1939), pp. 35-36 and references there.

in singing the first six verses. When the procession stands outside the city gate the chief musician leads in the antiphonal use of the last four verses. Time does not permit us to figure out the parts of the different voices and the various groups, doubtless including little children. The reader may allocate the various parts. If he does, let him assign to the tenor those appealing words "Who is the King of glory?" [3]

This majestic psalm lends itself to the uses of many a noteworthy public occasion. Some of us always choose these uplifting words for Palm Sunday. The Protestant Episcopal Church employs the song on Ascension Day, and the Greek Orthodox Church at the dedication of a new sanctuary. Whatever the setting, the Twenty-fourth Psalm reminds us that the character of our God determines the spirit of our worship. He is holy. He has revealed His power and His glory supremely in the Person of His Son. That must be what He wishes us to remember as we say together the triumphant words:

> The Lord of hosts,
> He is the King of glory.

2. *The folly of human interference* (vv. 6-11). Again the historian brings out one of his amazing contrasts. Here he shows how the most careful plans of men go awry. The most momentous day thus far in the career of King David had to be marred by an accident. At a difficult place in the roadway the oxen stumbled. The cart holding the Ark threatened to overturn. Impetuously a man named Uzzah reached forth to steady the tottering cart. Thus he lost his life. Probably the cart turned over and pinned him to earth. Whatever led to the death of Uzzah,

---

[3] See *The Psalms and Lamentations,* "The Modern Reader's Bible" series, ed. Richard G. Moulton (Macmillan, 1906), pp. 44-46, 190-93; also C. C. Keet and G. H. Box, *A Liturgical Study of the Psalter* (Macmillan, 1928), pp. 63-66, 94-96.

the Hebrew writer ascribed to God what we should attribute to secondary causes.

If Uzzah had stopped to think he would have known that he could not keep the cart from toppling over. He should have trusted the Lord to take care of the Ark without human interference. According to Hebrew law the Ark was to be carried only by men set apart for the priesthood. It was not to be touched by other human hands.[3] For us impetuous folk the record may serve as a warning. With the best of intentions, leaping to act before we pause to think, ofttimes we "interfere with the affairs of God's Kingdom, as though they were in peril and needed saving."

Theoretically, we may not all agree about why Uzzah died. Actually, we can see how that tragic event affected the program of King David. The fatality affected him so strongly that he abandoned his plans for the triumphal procession into the Holy City. Instead of all that ceremony, he caused the Ark to be left in the house of a farmer named Obed-edom. There the visible symbol of God's presence rested for three months. During that period the household enjoyed the favor of the Lord. To this very day "the house of Obed-edom" serves as an object lesson of the family circle that centers round the altar of God. There the members of the household receive His blessing. "By faith they meet around one common mercy seat."

3. *The setting up of the Ark in Jerusalem* (vv. 12-15). Again the annalist resorts to contrast. In fact, he employs what we call thesis, antithesis, and synthesis. The thesis relates to plans for bringing the Ark to the capital city. The antithesis concerns the miscarriage of those elaborate arrangements. The synthesis has to do with the later fulfillment of the ruler's dreams about the central sanctuary. Such a way of analyzing the record would

[4] See Num. 4:15; 8:6-9.

have astounded the Hebrew writer. Even so, we may pause to admire his unconscious skill as a dramatist.

Now for more facts. When David learned that God was blessing the home that sheltered the Ark, he went in person and fetched the Ark into Jerusalem. On the way to the city he led the people in offering sacrifices. He likewise made provision for music, and he showed his exultation in a sacred dance. His way of exposing his person seems strange to us now, and even unseemly, as it did then to his wife. As an Oriental he put his heart into his religion. As a man of his day he expressed his feelings in primitive forms. Before we begin to find fault with his "exhibitionism," let us ask ourselves if we have any overpowering emotions to express. According to the Bible, is not religion largely a matter of feeling? [5]

When the procession came into the city the Ark rested on the site of the future temple. Solomon's Temple is said to have been erected on the spot where Abraham had stood ready to offer up Isaac as a living sacrifice. All of this may signify little to us matter-of-fact Americans. But such holy associations loomed large in the eyes of the Hebrews. They would understand why the king sacrificed burnt offerings and peace offerings when he set up the Ark in Jerusalem. To the children of Israel burnt offerings symbolized renewed dedication to the service of God. Peace offerings expressed gratitude for His manifold blessings. For much the same reasons the king distributed royal largess in the way of good things to eat. He wished the people to look back on that day with thanksgiving and delight.

Let our discussion close with something practical. Every city or open countryside needs a local sanctuary. Near the heart of every neighborhood let there stand a visible symbol of God's indwelling Presence and His readiness to bless. Among all of

[5] See Jonathan Edwards, *A Treatise Concerning the Religious Affections*, Philadelphia, 1821.

David's contributions to the rebuilding of the nation, none could have proved more salutary than this way of putting religion at the center of the community life. On the other hand, the king must have known that the value of the symbol depended on the blessing of God. Hence he would have rejoiced in the words written by one of his descendants:

> Except the Lord build the house,
> They labor in vain that build it:
> Except the Lord keep the city,
> The watchman waketh but in vain.[6]

CHAPTER 27

THE DESIRE TO ERECT A SANCTUARY

II Samuel 7

THE SUBJECT OF THIS CHAPTER INTERESTS ALMOST EVERY CHURCH-man. Many a parish now faces the question of remodeling the old edifice or else tearing it down and building anew. Across the sea countless victims of bombs now clear away the debris. Then will follow the erection of new homes and church buildings, perhaps not so costly and elegant as before. Before we enter such an era of rebuilding let us pause to inquire what God thinks of our plans. While we cannot ask for blueprints from heaven to guide us brick by brick, we can discover principles that obtain wherever church folk build according to the pattern shown in the Mount.[1]

1. *The desire to build a house for God* (vv. 1-7). The Lord must have intended David to become a builder. Dearly did he love to make plans for a new structure and then to watch the walls arise. In the days of His flesh the Son of David likewise served as a builder. In the Epistles, Paul repeatedly writes about religion in terms of architecture. In fact, almost every normal man feels some such impulse of construction. Before anyone starts to build a church, however, let him be sure about his divine commission. Who but God can authorize any person to inaugurate a movement for the erection of a sanctuary? All of this and more we learn from the experience of David.

The king's motives seemed worthy of praise. He felt that he should not reside in a more stately edifice than the one that

---

[1] See Phillips Brooks, "The Pattern in the Mount," *Sermons,* III, 1-21.

sheltered the Ark. Down in his heart David must have been a lover of peace. He must have longed to use his time and strength in meeting the needs of men. Above all did he wish to worship in an attractive sanctuary. Before he took any steps in that direction, however, he conferred with the public representative of God. From the lips of the prophet he received the heartiest approval. When has a forward-looking "minister" such as Nathan ever frowned on the desire of his leading layman to erect a stately sanctuary?

Nathan here comes before us for the first time. Like many another "pastoral counselor," this one gives unwise advice. Where a prudent physician would wait until he was sure of the diagnosis, the man of God decides offhand, with no reservations. "Go, do all that is in thy heart; for the Lord is with thee." But that same night, perhaps when he took time to pray, Nathan learned the folly of his snap judgment. Even a spiritual-minded prophet could not be sure about his opinions until he had submitted them to God.

The next time this man appears before us he commits no such blunder. When he appears in the presence of the king to utter words of rebuke, the prophet speaks with a sense of finality. Wherein lies the difference between the two occasions? Apparently, when Nathan advises the king to build, the prophet speaks before he has prayed. But afterward, when he confronts a heinous sinner and speaks to his conscience, the seer has a mandate from the court of Heaven. Is there no need of such an interpreter now? "Thus saith the Lord!" "When a message comes from God to a man, he needn't ask if it's true!"

As for the proposal to build the temple, why did the Lord not approve the project? The narrative does not explain the reason. The record simply makes clear that God withheld His sanction. He had never expressed a desire for David to erect such a sanctuary. And yet the Lord planned for the building of that temple! Evidently the objection to David had to do with his exploits as a warrior. Elsewhere he is reported to have told "all the princes of Israel": "God said unto me, Thou shalt not build a house for my name, because thou art a man of war, and hast shed blood."[2] For much the same reason the Lord's people now would hesitate to name a sanctuary after such a hero as Admiral Nimitz or General Eisenhower.

Our Lord wishes to choose the man who will erect the new sanctuary. Since the wars of David are not ended, prudence would suggest that the field general postpone his plans for building a church. However, he can busy himself with collecting the materials to be used some day by his son and heir. That future monarch will be known as a man of peace. Can we not infer that the Church of God should stand as a memorial to peace rather than war? Is this why some of us when in London have felt more at home in St. Paul's than at Westminster Abbey?

2. *The promise of a sure house for King David* (vv. 8-17). When God withholds one blessing, He has a way of granting another, and that more glorious. Instead of permitting the king to erect a new church edifice, the Lord promises that his household shall endure and become a means of blessing to the world. Here the stress falls on what God plans to do for David, not on what David wishes to do for God. In keeping with the grandeur of these promises, the style soars into realms of rarest beauty. Where even in the twin books of Samuel can one find a more moving prose rhythm?

Four brief sayings call for special notice. Each has to do with what Lord Tweedsmuir terms "The King's Grace," or God's way of dispensing His royal bounty. The first of the sayings relates to the past: "I took thee." The King's grace has shown itself in choosing the shepherd lad to become ruler of the elect nation. The second saying concerns the period between that in-

[2] I Chron. 28:1, 3; cf. I Kings 5:3.

itial choice and the present hour: "I have been with thee." What more could the heart of man desire? The third and fourth look toward the unknown future: "I will make thee a great name"; and "I will appoint a place for my people Israel, and will plant them."

Still other glowing promises concern the dynasty that the king has established. His descendants will erect that edifice of which David has only dreamed. They will become known among men as kings. Indeed their dominion will endure forever. The word "forever" seems to dominate the entire passage. Partly for this reason many scholars look on the words as pointing to the coming Redeemer.[3] Some interpreters regard this as the most important of all the Messianic predictions concerning Christ as the Son of David. Hence the passage calls for loving study, in the spirit of prayer.

The Lord says that He will establish His Kingdom and make it endure forever. This assurance He gives in various forms, direct and indirect. To a limited degree the promises doubtless refer to Solomon and his successors on the throne. But to us as Christians the predictions reach far beyond those earthly rulers. We believe that the facts about King David and his son afford the framework in which the Hebrew seer beheld the glory of the coming Redeemer. Even today many of those promises await fulfillment. Thus far we have not seen all things put under His feet. But still we behold Him who alone can claim to be King of Kings. Also we contend for "the crown rights of the Redeemer."

3. *The prayer for a blessing on the king's house* (vv. 18-29). How does David respond to these overtures of mercy? When he learns that he must not even start to build the temple, does he

---

[3] See Charles A. Briggs, *Messianic Prophecy* (Scribner's, 1891), pp. 126-32; and Willis J. Beecher, *The Prophets and the Promise* (Crowell, 1905), pp. 228-40.

feel disgruntled and aggrieved? No! On the contrary, he prays. He does not once allude to the edifice that he has planned to erect. Thus the Bible paragraph brings to light the best thing we know about King David. That is greatness of soul. Since his heart has been strangely warmed, his words of prayer flow in a beautiful rhythm. Nowhere else in the Old Testament can we find a nobler example of how to pray on a special occasion.[4]

Like almost every prayer in the Bible, this one voices feeling rather than thought. The heart of the suppliant pours out its deepest desires. David rests in the assurance that God too can feel. As Browning would sing, "O heart I made, a heart beats here." In the presence of the Most High the king humbles himself. He expresses a sense of personal unworthiness. Nevertheless, he shows himself willing to receive all that the Lord stands ready to bestow. Thus the prayer moves through adoration and thanksgiving to supplication for the continued favor of God. After such a reading who does not feel impelled to cry out, "Lord, teach me to pray"?

This prayer reminds us that here on earth the Kingdom of God centers largely in the home. When we started into this chapter from Samuel we were thinking about a church edifice to be fashioned out of wood and stone. Now we should be far more intent on the Christ of the Church, and on His coming to earth through the believing home. In this spirit let us pray for the family circle that is dearest to our hearts. "It does not matter so much what sort of house people dwell in, as what sort of people dwell in the house."

Who then will dare to make his own the closing words of King David? "Bless the house of thy servant, that it may continue for ever before thee; for thou, O Lord God, hast spoken it: and with thy blessing let the house of thy servant be blessed for ever."

[4] See John E. McFadyen, *The Prayers of the Bible* (Armstrong, 1906), pp. 197-220.

CHAPTER 28

THE KINDNESS OF A CONQUEROR

II Samuel 9

THIS PASSAGE BRINGS OUT THE GOOD SIDE OF KING DAVID'S PERSON-
ality. When his heart had its way, as it often did, he could be
tender and kind, even magnanimous. In the scene at hand he
went out of his way to show concern for any surviving descend-
ant of King Saul. Thus again David set an example of how to
heal wounds caused by fratricidal strife. In various respects,
therefore, he deserved some such title as "Greatheart."

1. *The motive for being kind* (vv. 1-8). Why should the king
have taken the initiative in searching for descendants of Saul?
Did not the incoming ruler have enough to do in straightening
out the affairs of the kingdom? Perhaps he foresaw that the work
of rebuilding would proceed more surely if the new ruler secured
justice for those in distress and mercy for those in need. If so,
he must have learned that the welfare of the nation depended
largely on the well-being of its people, one by one. In this respect,
at least, King David resembled God. Has not the Heavenly
Father gone far out of His way to show us kindness as well as
justice?

> There's a kindness in His justice,
> Which is more than liberty.

Listen, then, to King David: "Is there yet any that is left of
the house of Saul, that I may show him kindness for Jonathan's
sake?" Here we learn something vital about "the King's grace."
In the biblical sense of the term, grace means divine goodness to
the unworthy. Grace does not concern itself with a man's deserts

so much as with his needs. By way of return it asks that the one in need accept the proffered gift and use it well. On the human level, something akin to the grace of God appeared in King David. He showed kindness to a helpless cripple without stopping to ask whether or not he was worthy.

This truth comes out whimsically in *Hamlet*. Loquacious old Polonius in the second act says about the visiting players: "I will use them according to their desert." The Prince of Denmark replies: "Man, much better: use every man after his desert, and who should 'scape whipping? Use them after your own worth and dignity: the less they deserve, the more merit is in your bounty."

As for David, his motive appears in the words "for Jonathan's sake." In youth the future king had entered into a covenant of friendship with the son of Saul.[1] That covenant of kindness included both men, as well as their offspring. Because of David's love for Jonathan, Mephibosheth received kindnesses that he seems not to have merited. In that turbulent and bloody era David might have contented himself with dealing out justice, more or less impersonally. Why did he not let all men fare alike? Because of that covenant with Jonathan, the king's heart went out to the crippled son of his deceased friend.

Mephibosheth seems to have had only two claims for special attention: he was the son of Jonathan, and was lame in both feet. At the age of five years, just after his father and grandfather were slain, the child was dropped from his nurse's arms and made a cripple for life. Perhaps for that reason, his personality seems to have been warped. Because of his infirmity he may have developed an inferiority complex. Whatever the inside story about supposed later machinations against King David, Mephibosheth the cripple enjoyed the favor and the bounty of his father's dearest friend.

[1] See I Sam. 18:1-3; 20:8-17, 42.

These facts once led to a so-called sermon of the kind that has brought "doctrinal preaching" into disrepute. Whatever the text or subject of his harangue, a certain parson always tried to display his entire system of theological dogmas. One morning when he announced his text the long-suffering people breathed a sigh of relief. How could he find his pet teachings in words about a cripple?—"Mephibosheth dwelt in Jerusalem. . . . And he was lame in both his feet."

The dear old doctor, however, "froze to the occasion"! One by one he trotted out the same old stand-bys. In sepulchral tones he proclaimed that the lameness of Mephibosheth indicated natural depravity, his being crippled in both feet showed total depravity, his dwelling at Jerusalem signified justification by faith, his eating at the king's table pointed to adoption, and his being there continually taught the final perseverance of the saints. When rightly understood, all of these truths commend themselves to many of us, but they do not appear in the present passage. It shows a ruler's kindness to a cripple, for his father's sake. When shall we ministers quit twisting the Scriptures?

2. *The bounty of the king's kindness* (vv. 9-13). Because of David's love for Jonathan, Mephibosheth inherited the estate of King Saul, with all its revenues. The cripple likewise enjoyed the privilege of sitting daily at the royal table. These two marks of distinction went together. Symbolically, they showed that he stood in favor at the court. No one but a helpless cripple in the Near East could appreciate what these prerogatives meant to the recipient. Incidentally, they must have given him a new sense of security. As long as he lived in the mansion of the king, crippled Mephibosheth would escape the assassin's dagger.

In terms of our day, what did that cripple enjoy? Four blessings that seldom abound in the Near East: freedom from want and freedom from fear, freedom of speech and freedom to worship. Whether or not he took advantage of his new liberties, no one can say. At any rate, he had all that heart could desire to make him comfortable and happy. That is what underprivileged folk everywhere are crying for today. However unattractive in appearance and personality, however warped and embittered by pain and shame, anyone who suffers from a mental or physical handicap needs a friend who will be kind "for Jonathan's sake."

What has the benefactor a right to expect in return? Loyalty and gratitude. In both respects King David met with disappointment. Later in his career, just when he most needed friendship and support, the king had reason to suspect that Mephibosheth had become a traitor.[2] Perhaps these suspicions had little foundation in fact. The cripple blamed all the delinquencies on Ziba, his man of affairs. More probably, both Mephibosheth and Ziba were at fault. If so, their way of returning evil for good makes us think of how we mortals treat God.

From the passage as a whole we may draw a parallel. However, let us remember that it can be nothing more. We think of David's kindness to that cripple as resembling the Father's goodness to a sinner. In the New Testament we find no warrant for making such a comparison. Still we love to think of our God's kindness to us mortals, one by one, because of the covenant with His Son who died for us all. How have we responded to God's overtures of mercy? Much as Mephibosheth seems to have treated David. Occasionally we have rebelled. More often we have misused the tokens of God's favor. If so, let us fall down before Him and plead for mercy. Then we shall find that He has never forgotten the covenant of grace. How can we ever thank Him for such royal bounty? [3]

[2] See II Sam. 16:1-4; 19:17, 29-30.
[3] The section II Samuel 9-20 contains some of the noblest Hebrew prose. In English, too, the style is worthy of study.

CHAPTER 29

THE TEMPTATIONS OF MIDDLE AGE

II Samuel 11

DO WE MINISTERS DEVOTE SUFFICIENT ATTENTION TO THE PERILS OF middle age? Do we, indeed, think of them at all when we prepare for the pulpit? Often we hold forth about the pitfalls of the young. Sometimes we consider the plight of the old. But we forget about the perils in "the middle passage of the years."

For example, think of David. Look on him as perhaps fifty years of age. Remember that if he had died in battle when forty-nine he would have gone down in history as a hero without a blot on the escutcheon. Imagine how he would have served as an object lesson of all the manly virtues. Then recall those words of the Almighty to the prophet Samuel: "Man looketh on the outward appearance, but the Lord looketh on the heart."

Why did King David fall? Perhaps because of a change in his lifelong habits. Throughout the years he had spent his waking hours in the open air. He had kept his hands clean, because he had kept them busy. But when he tried to exist for a year within the four walls of a city, he soon fell into sin. All through his earlier career, at times, he may have dallied with thoughts of evil. Only when he became idle did he fall into the depths of iniquity.

1. *The appeal to a man's baser self* (vv. 1-5). After he had passed the zenith of life the king became the most notorious sinner of his day, if not in all Hebrew history. Deliberately and without excuse he committed a series of the most dastardly sins that a human being can perpetrate. First he fell into adultery. In as far as the record shows, he bore the whole blame.

He did not yield to the blandishments and bewitching wiles of some Delilah. He looked on a beautiful woman and lusted after her. Then he carried his sinful desires into action. From this one sin he went on to others. Thus he started an endless chain of iniquity.

Why does such a man appear in the Hebrew Hall of Fame? Or rather, why do his transgressions loom large in the Bible? One of his own people must have penned our vivid account of the king's enormities. Whatever the reason for including these facts, the blackness of the record makes us feel that it must be true. It may even induce a feeling of relief. If God could pardon and bless such a deliberate sinner as David, who among us need despair? Our transgressions in middle age may differ from those of the king. Even so, let him that is without sin among us cast the first stone at adulterous David.

2. *The attempt to escape from the consequences of sin* (vv. 6-13). Here again the narrative shows how human nature runs true to form. When the king learned that the woman in the case was expecting a babe, how did he feel? Did he show any sense of shame, not to speak of remorse? No, for his conscience seems to have fallen asleep. He simply tried to cover up his wrongdoing and thus escape the aftermath. Such a state of heart reminds us of the apostle's words about consciences branded with a hot iron.[1] Whatever the figure means, it points to the secret of many a sin. Whenever a man's conscience fails to work, he sinks deeper and deeper into the mire. Who but God can deliver him then?

3. *The resort to political trickery* (vv. 14-21). Whenever a king has committed an "indiscretion" he can bring to his aid all the forces of the royal court. He can command his henchmen to hush up the scandal. But poor David did not succeed. Perhaps he had never learned how to manage such intrigues. He may have failed to reckon with the woman's husband. How could the

---

[1] I Tim. 4:2*b*.

king foresee that this other veteran of the wars would refuse to become known as the father of the king's child? In time the monarch had to devise stern measures for dealing with the perverse fellow. Would that David had shown like perseverance in the pursuit of righteousness!

4. *The sin of indirect murder* (vv. 22-25). Such a brilliant tactician as David could think of more than one way to "liquidate" an undesirable soldier. The scheme that the king devised left him clear in the eyes of the law. As long as his conscience failed to condemn, what had he to dread? After he had caused the woman's husband to fall in battle, the royal culprit might have whispered to himself, with a sigh of relief: "All's well that ends well!" Perhaps so, if a man forgets God. For years this one had stood out in his world as the public representative of the Most High. Indeed, he was to become the forebear of the promised Messiah. And yet the most highly favored of men had deliberately committed adultery and murder. Worse still, he had no thought of confessing those sins. What can the Almighty do with such an ingrate?

For a parallel case turn again to *Hamlet*. The incoming king of Denmark has seduced Hamlet's mother and slain her husband, so as to steal the crown. One of the most moving scenes in the tragic drama shows how the king strives to shrive his soul. This passage throws light on what we call "unanswered prayers." Why insist on calling them prayers? Listen to the prattling of the king, who has not sought pardon and cleansing from God:

> O, my offence is rank, it smells to heaven;
> It hath the primal eldest curse upon 't,
> A brother's murder! Pray can I not.
>
> . . . .
>
> What if this cursed hand
> Were thicker than itself with brother's blood,

Is there not rain enough in the sweet heavens
To wash it white as snow? . . .

. . . .

I am still possess'd
Of those effects for which I did the murder,
My crown, mine own ambition, and my queen.
May one be pardon'd and retain the offence?

. . . .

Bow, stubborn knees; and, heart with strings of steel,
Be soft as sinews of the new-born babe.

Here the adulterous, murderous king retires and kneels. A little
later he rises and says with a sigh:

My words fly up, my thoughts remain below:
Words without thoughts never to heaven go.

5. *The condemnation from God* (vv. 26-27). After his indirect
murder of the woman's husband, David took her as his wife.
If by so doing he hoped to escape the consequences of sin, he
soon discovered his error. The culprit still had to face the Supreme Court: "The thing that David had done displeased the
Lord." When a man of middle years, "the heir of all the ages,"
has stooped to commit adultery and murder, how can he escape
the righteous judgment of God?

How does the Lord arouse the conscience that has refused to
function in the face of unspeakable sin? Sometimes God uses
preaching in the sanctuary. More often, as in the present case,
He employs "pastoral counseling." When the leading layman
in the kingdom has fallen into the grossest sins, what will the
man of God say and do? Will he speak out in the name of his
Lord, or will he hold his peace? For an object lesson of ministerial
tact and courage look at Nathan the prophet.

Let there be still another word about the man of middle

213

years. The ideal for this perilous stage appears in a tale of adventure by Lord Tweedsmuir. The closing words come from a man no longer young: "I seem to learn the lesson of the years. ... Deep in it all, more clear as the hours pass and the wrappings fall off, shines forth the golden star of honor, which, if a man follow, though it be through quagmire and desert, fierce fires and poignant sorrow, 'twill bring him at length to a place of peace." [2]

[2] John Buchan, *John Burnet of Barns* (Dodd, Mead, 1924), p. **317.**

CHAPTER 30

THE APPEAL TO A MAN'S CONSCIENCE

II Samuel 12

THE PROPHET NATHAN SHOWS HOW TO REACH A STRONG MAN'S CONscience. Really the seer acted as a personal counselor, but for the present we may think of him as a preacher. When he spoke to the King, Nathan knew that he was addressing a monarch who had deliberately committed adultery and murder. How would the prophet deal with the culprit? Would the preacher dodge the issue, strike out straight from the shoulder, or use God-given imagination and tact? Nathan chose the latter course. He must have prayed to God before he spoke to man. Even as literature this appeal to conscience ranks high. Here it will serve as an object lesson of how to preach for a verdict.

1. *The parable about the lamb* (vv. 1-6). We are now to study one of the two parables in the Old Testament.[1] Not even in the New Testament can we find anything more exquisite. When Dean Luther A. Weigle of Yale lectured at another seminary about our Lord as teacher, the crowning example came from this parable. The few simple words from Nathan embody what we call a "psychological approach." This means beginning with your hearer where you find him and then leading him gradually to accept the truth of God. All of this Nathan accomplished, largely because of the way he began. He knew what lay close to the heart of the shepherd king.

"The poor man had nothing, save one little ewe lamb." What a way to reach the heart of a shepherd! Note how the speaker

[1] For the other parable see Isa. 5:1-7.

singled out one little lamb and not a flock of full-grown sheep. For much the same reason our Lord phrased many of His parables in the singular. He spoke about the house on the rock and the house on the sand, the lost sheep and the lost coin, as well as the lost son. At least until recently, some of us social-minded pulpiteers would have inveighed against "the gigantic evils of the Packers' Trust in its mercenary monopolistic attitudes toward the defenseless sheepmen of the remote Northwest." Why not learn from Nathan and our Lord how to present truth so as to reach the conscience?

From another point of view the stress in the parable falls on the owner of the ewe lamb. Here too the master of words leads us to see a single person. He has suffered a serious wrong at the hands of the king. As often elsewhere, the Scriptures show the duty of a man to a man. Instead of emphasizing the claims of the underprivileged masses, the Bible emphasis usually falls on the rights of a single person. What Horace Bushnell used to term "the individualizing power" has characterized almost every first-class preacher from Paul and Peter to Robertson and Spurgeon, Bushnell and Brooks. In the pulpit such a man of God quickly leads the hearer to become a seer.

2. *The meaning of the parable* (vv. 7-12). The effectiveness of such preaching appears in the response of the hearer. The parable aroused the ire of the king against the rich man who had done the wrong. Then came the proof of the preacher's courage: "Thou art the man!" That sounds like John Knox before Queen Mary, or like Bourdaloue before Louis XIV. Such an appeal to the conscience must be direct, manly, heart-searching. "The word of God is quick, and powerful, and sharper than any twoedged sword, piercing." [2] Is there no call for such pulpit work today? Listen to a strong theologian in England:

[2] Heb. 4:12 (A.V.).

216

Anything that minimizes the impression that the preacher is speaking directly to the individual listener, as man to man, . . . is to be avoided. Do not be afraid to use the pronoun "You," which is our common usage for "Thou." . . . It would be wearisome to speak thus in the second person right through the sermon; indeed it is impossible if there is any development of a theme. Moreover, used persistently and in the wrong way, it might give the impression of nagging or browbeating, and of the preacher setting himself up on a pedestal. Yet such direct address should never be entirely omitted. If there is no place where you can say "You," then it is strongly to be suspected that your discourse is not a sermon but a lecture or an essay.[3]

3. *The forgiveness of deadly sins* (v. 13). As soon as the prophet had spoken a few words, to make clear the truth of the parable, David confessed his sin: "I have sinned against the Lord." What could be more manly, more personal, more lowly? "I have sinned . . . I alone am to blame . . . *I have sinned against the Lord.*" David might have insisted that he had been tempted beyond his power to resist. He might have referred to his foibles and his lapses. But no. He had sinned, and that against the Holy One who had poured out upon the king blessings too many and too vast for him to receive. In full view of what he had done against the home of Uriah, and against the fatherland, still the conscience-stricken king felt most of all the offenses against God:

> Against thee, thee only, have I sinned,
> And done that which is evil in thy sight.[4]

David's confession of sin led to an immediate assurance of pardon. Only a little while before, the king had exclaimed: "The

[3] Herbert H. Farmer, *The Servant of the Word* (Scribner, 1942), pp. 63-64.

[4] Psa. 51:4. For two other studies in the forgiveness of sins, turn to Psalms 51 and 32, in this order. Whoever wrote those songs of penitence must have entered into fellowship with all that David suffered before he found pardon and peace.

man that hath done this is worthy to die!" David's outburst concerned the overlord who had stolen a poor man's lamb. How much more swiftly should judgment fall on the king who had stolen a soldier's wife and then had slain her husband! Nevertheless, when the culprit confessed his sins he received forgiveness, once and forever. He did not have to endure the throes of penance. Even if he had striven to right those wrongs, what could he have done? All that even a monarch could do was to cast himself on the mercy of God.

David must have known that the Hebrew religion provided no sacrifices for such presumptuous sins. Still he found pardon, cleansing, and peace. His forgiveness was immediate: "The Lord ... hath put away thy sin." It was complete, and it was permanent. Never again would he have to plead for mercy because of those evils that he could not forget. He could claim the promise that those transgressions would be remembered against him no more for ever. His experience brings us to the heart of the gospel in the Old Testament. Whenever the vilest of men casts himself on the mercy of God, he can sing with the psalmist:

> Blessed is he whose transgression is forgiven,
> Whose sin is covered.
>
> . . . .
>
> Be glad in the Lord, and rejoice, ye righteous;
> And shout for joy, all ye that are upright in heart.[5]

4. The aftereffects of forgiven sins (vv. 14-23). "Whatsoever a man soweth, that shall he also reap." [6] Unfortunately, the reaping of wild oats may continue long after a man of middle age has repented and found forgiveness. In the case of King David the

---

[5] Psa. 32:1, 11. Both Psalm 32 and Psalm 51 are traditionally ascribed to King David. The latter deals with prayer for pardon, the former with thanksgiving after forgiveness.

[6] Gal. 6:7b.

reaping began with the death of the child conceived in sin. When the babe fell sick and seemed ready to die, the grief-stricken father fasted and prayed. But after the little one had ceased to breathe, the father went back to his daily tasks. His saying about the child deserves immortality. It shows how near the Old Testament can come to the Christian teaching about life everlasting: "I shall go to him, but he will not return to me."

Giving up his child proved to be only the first of the king's woes. During all the rest of his days on earth he had to reap a harvest of sorrow and shame. He had to witness among his sons and daughters the very same sins he had shown them how to commit. Could he hope to hold them back from incest, from murder, and from disloyalty to the fatherland? Could he tell them how he had found pardon, cleansing, and peace? Do a man's sins ever look so black as when he sees them reproduced in his sons and daughters? Let every man of middle age beware lest he spend his remaining years reaping a harvest of woe from his forgiven sins.

This Bible passage affords materials for a moving drama. According to a student of the art, a sacred drama calls for a few persons in action that appeals to the eye of the onlooker.[7] The action involves conflict, or struggle, which causes increasing suspense, and leads up to an exciting climax. The appeal througnout comes more and more to the emotions. All of this emerges in the narrative about King David's sins and God's forgiveness. Why do we ministers not learn how to make the Scriptures live and move?

"Not until the modern pulpit is willing to take the trouble to understand how poets, artists, painters, and musicians work," says Willard L. Sperry, "will the art of preaching come again into

---

[7] See Fred Eastman, "The Dramatist and the Minister," in *The Arts and Religion*, pp. 135-69.

its own."[8] When the art of preaching comes again into its own, we shall have in the pulpit more of masculine strength and more of preaching to the conscience. "In the conscience," says James Stalker, "the battle is to be won or lost. . . . He will never be a preacher who does not know how to get at the conscience. . . . How should he know who has not himself a keen sense of honour and an awful reverence for moral purity?"[9]

[8] *Reality in Worship* (Macmillan, 1925), p. 248.
[9] *The Preacher and His Models* (Armstrong, 1892), p. 156.

CHAPTER 31

THE WILES OF AN UNWORTHY SON

II Samuel 15

THE AFTEREFFECTS OF DAVID'S FORGIVEN SINS APPEAR STARTLINGLY in his son Absalom. The father had been guilty of adultery, scheming, murder, and disloyalty to the fatherland. He had disrupted the home of a loyal soldier and had done much to break down the morale of countless other households. After David repented and found forgiveness, he began to suffer in his own family circle the very same wrongs he had inflicted on other families. What a harvest of wild oats!

This tragic drama unfolds by definite stages. The thirteenth chapter of Second Samuel recounts the sin of incest. One of David's sons lusted after his half-sister, and would not rest until he had defiled her person. Then he thrust her away as though she were a thing of shame. Thus he incurred the undying enmity of Absalom, on whom the spotlight falls. As the full brother of the princess who had been defiled, Absalom began to contrive ways and means for avenging her shame. His trickery here reminds us of David's schemes for doing away with the husband of Bath-sheba. After two whole years Absalom compassed the death of the half-brother who had been guilty of incest. Thus the sacred writer introduces the prince who will try to steal his father's throne. Now let us turn to the fifteenth chapter.

1. *The way to win men's hearts* (vv. 1-6). Young Absalom must have known that the Hebrew people deserved to be called the children of Israel. In sooth, he found them childish. Himself the son of a former shepherd, the young fellow must have

221

regarded them as silly sheep. He could see that with the right sort of leader they would seldom go astray. But he foresaw that they would quickly succumb to the blandishments of a shrewd demagogue. Since we in the States elect our rulers, we do well to study the ways of this unscrupulous politician. Sometimes the same sly spirit sneaks into the Church.

Like many another schemer in Church or State, Absalom possessed the gifts and graces that constitute personality, or charm. "In all Israel there was none to be so much praised as Absalom for his beauty; from the sole of his foot even to the crown of his head there was no blemish in him." Especially did he take pride in his hair. All in all, he might have sat as the subject for a word painting by Shakespeare: "What a piece of work is a man! how noble in reason! how infinite in faculty! in form and moving how express and admirable! in action how like an angel! in apprehension how like a god! the beauty of the world! the paragon of animals!"

In these glowing phrases the stress falls on the word at the end. Absalom seems to have been a beautiful beast. A schemer of this type appreciates the importance of self-display. He cultivates all the arts and wiles of the showman. Hence young Absalom secured horses and a chariot, with fifty men to run before him, as though he were a king. Behold him as he drives up to the city gates. Note how he salutes every citizen who comes in from the country with a "chip on his shoulder." Irrespective of the facts in the case, the schemer tells how he would redress such wrongs if he were king. All of this sounds like a typical city boss today. He promises everything golden in the way of utopia, and then he sugar-coats his lies with the sweetest of flatteries. Of course he takes from the public purse the funds to make possible his display and his largess.

Thus Absalom "stole" the hearts of the people. The same Hebrew verb appears in Genesis, where Rachel is said to have stolen her father's idols; and in Exodus, where everyone is warned: "Thou shalt not steal." In order to steal the hearts of people en masse, a politician needs to have skill as well as charm. In our own early history all of that held true of Aaron Burr. Today in Princeton Cemetery his body lies buried at the foot of his grandfather's grave. The grandfather, Jonathan Edwards, might have shown the young fellow how to use his gifts and graces in the service of God and men. But at the age of twenty-one Burr is said deliberatively to have turned away from the religion of his fathers. Erelong he began publicly to steal the hearts of men, as privately he had been seducing their daughters. Today he serves as an object lesson of brilliant powers worse than wasted. What does such a schemer lack save character?

2. *The way to start a rebellion* (vv. 7-12). The word "rebellion" refers to an open insurrection against the powers that be in the land. Usually the term points to an uprising that has failed. Such was the case with the movement under Aaron Burr. The facts about his scheme are far from clear. He may have been unwise rather than disloyal. But there can be no question about Absalom. He strove to usurp his father's throne. Both in laying his plans and in carrying them out the young upstart showed uncanny ability. Except for lack of character he stood out as a "man born to be king."

Such a schemer knows the value of strategy. Absalom chose to disguise his undertaking under the garb of religion. With no piety of his own, he felt sure that such a cloak would deceive King David. The same sort of cunning led Absalom to select the scene for his uprising. Well did he know that in Hebron David had once begun a spectacular career as king, and that the city had become associated with the exploits of the ruler before he grew old. Thus the upstart planned to make the insurrection look like the uprising of irresistible youth against futile old age.

Do you wonder that Absalom almost succeeded in usurping his father's throne?

Over against the young scoundrel's strategy think of his followers' simplicity. In the worthy sense of the term, simplicity would be pleasing to God. But a certain type of "simple simplicity" opens the way for the wiles of the demagogue. It succumbs to the splendor of spectacular showmanship, and likewise swallows all sorts of impossible promises. No matter how often childish folk have been deceived and led astray, they stand ready to follow any plausible aspirant for their votes and their service. Fortunately, more than a few of our citizens refuse to be fooled by any such demagogue. Otherwise there might be little hope for our democracy.

A popular uprising against the government makes a strong appeal to any man with a grudge. That may have been why Ahithophel became one of Absalom's right-hand men. Ahithophel seems to have been the grandfather of the woman whom David had seduced. If so, Ahithophel must have felt that the country needed another king. How could that grandfather remain loyal to adulterous David? So must other men of influence have fallen away from the king after his series of deadly sins. They must have felt that the time had come for a clean slate, even at the cost of blood. Perhaps so, but why succumb to the wiles of Absalom?

3. *The way to meet such wiles* (vv. 13-37). The remainder of chapter 15 tells how the king met this unexpected peril. Since it caught him unprepared, he was forced to flee. Even in flight he met with loyal support in unlikely quarters. After his son had turned traitor and had enlisted many others whom the king held dear, David found a strong helper in a foreigner named Ittai. Never does a leader value personal devotion so much as when everyone who matters seems to have gone over to the enemy. Ittai's assurances of fealty to harassed David remind us of the king's great-grandmother, an immigrant named Ruth. Did

she not pledge undying devotion to an older person who at the moment seemed down and out? [1]

The words of Ittai the immigrant must have brought new courage and strength to the fleeing king: "As the Lord liveth, and as my lord the king liveth, surely in what place my lord the king shall be, whether for death or for life, even there also will thy servant be." Loyalty of that sort comes close to the spirit of our religion. Even on its upper levels what does religion mean save loyalty to God and His Kingdom?

The biblical narrative likewise shows how the fleeing king planned to meet guile with guile. He knew that young Absalom would hasten to occupy Jerusalem, and that he would have at his right hand cunning Ahithophel. In order to circumvent the maneuvers of that vengeful adviser, David left behind him a number of loyal supporters. He bade them keep him informed about the progress of the insurrection. He also told them how to thwart the schemes of Ahithophel. Evidently the king had retained much of his old-time magnetism. But he seems to have lost something of his buoyancy. From this time onward, whether he is fleeing from the hosts of Absalom, or else waiting for tidings from the field of battle, David will seem like an aging man with a broken heart.

In view of all these facts, what shall we conclude? Simply this: if we would have the right sort of rulers tomorrow, we must have the right sort of fathers and sons today. What then are we doing in home and church to insure a sufficient number of leaders for Church and State? How else can we hope to prevent the rise of such a demagogue as Absalom? Both in Church and in State let us beware of the godless politician. Let us also encourage every father of a growing boy to be a Christian for the sake of his son.

---

[1] See Ruth 1:16-17; 4:17-21.

CHAPTER 32

THE GRIEF OF A VICTORIOUS FATHER

II Samuel 18

No MORE EXQUISITE TALE HAS EVER BEEN WRITTEN. CHARLES S. Baldwin says of it:

> This story, though it is part of a long history, is complete in itself. . . . That is the first requisite of a good story. It must be complete and entire, not a fragment, but a whole. . . . This story of one day in David's life teaches us, first of all, to tell one story at a time. It urges us, whenever we claim people's attention, to fix their attention on one particular point of interest, which we have settled beforehand, and which will make the story, whether it be long or short, stand out distinctly as complete in itself.[1]

These are the words of a professor at Columbia University. He is writing for students of English, and he is not concerned with religion. In the chapter "How to Tell a Story" he takes as his first example the passage now in hand. He praises the Hebrew author's ability to fix attention on one person; to let the tale have one chief event; to begin at the right point; to secure increasing intensity; and to have a moving climax, which may be tremendous. In short, making a story means cutting out "a little piece from the unending roll of life." All of this may well apply to preaching.

The Hebrew author must have been far more concerned about the meaning of his words than about their literary form. His own

[1] *The English Bible as a Guide to Writing* (Macmillan, 1917), pp. 110-12, *et al.*

heart must have been moved by the spectacle of that wartime father with his breaking heart. Doubtless the annalist had often told this tale at the campfire under the Judean stars. By noting the response of his hearers he had learned what to stress and what to omit. Somehow he had attained the distinction of art that calls no attention to itself. Today his story holds special interest for everyone who has awaited tidings from an unseen battlefield. Throughout the present study, keep your eyes fixed upon that father.

1. *The suspense of a wartime father* (vv. 1-5). Ever since the beginning of the insurrection, the king has been looking forward to this day of battle. Whichever way the tide may turn, the father's heart will be full of grief. His beloved son has become the leader of a rebellion against the land that gave him birth. If the young upstart meets with defeat, he will be slain, or else taken captive, in disgrace. If the son falls into the hands of bloodthirsty warriors bent on revenge, David knows how they will maltreat the handsome scoundrel. On the contrary, if the battle goes against the forces of the king, he and all his hopes for days to come will go a-glimmering. Worst of all, David feels that he himself has brought on this day of doom.

The troopers around the king do not share his tender feelings for Absalom. They look on the young upstart as the most despicable traitor in Hebrew history, and not merely as the spoiled darling of their aging king. They are so much concerned about the welfare of the father that they will not let him go out to battle: "Thou art worth ten thousand of us." Meantime how can they know what anguish fills his heart? How can rough and ruthless warriors share that grief because Absalom has followed in the footsteps of his father?

Much the same motif runs through a novel by Sinclair Lewis. His book *Prodigal Parents*[2] has never become popular, especially

[2] Doubleday, Doran, 1938.

among fathers and mothers. They might enjoy a thrilling tale about some prodigal son or daughter. But most of them draw the line against any volume that points to the cause in prodigal parents. Perhaps, too, the novelist might have achieved more success if he had singled out some one father, instead of having two. Why did he not study the Hebrew tale and learn from it "how to tell a story"?

From the troops about him poor David received no sympathy. In fact, he had to endure the taunts of rough old Joab, who was to command the forces of the king: "Thou lovest them that hate thee, and hatest them that love thee." If the grief-stricken king had been able to reply he might have exclaimed: "You forget that I am a father! Should a father ever cease to love his boy?" In our recent past almost every man of middle years tasted the bitter suspense of waiting for tidings from a battlefield. But who among us ever had a son in command of enemy forces? When has any modern author composed such a tragic tale as this one from life?

2. *The death of a rebellious son* (vv. 6-18). Instead of going out to witness the battle, let us tarry with David as he stands by some "gate-side" and waits for tidings. Late in the day of strife the reports begin to come in. The fighting has taken place in the forest of Ephraim, where the woods have devoured more soldiers than the sword could slay. But the king does not know that those victims have included Absalom. In the branches of a wide-spreading oak his son was caught by his head. There he hung between heaven and earth, unfit for either. In Bible school and at home we used to be told that he was caught by his hair. If so, those long flowing locks on which he prided himself became a sort of hangman's noose. Never again would that handsome scoundrel pose as "the glass of fashion and the mold of form, the observed of all observers."

What will be the fate of the young rascal as he hangs suspended from a tree? When the troops went out to battle this morning the king commanded Joab and the other warriors: "Deal gently for my sake with the young man"; and "Beware that none touch the young man Absalom." These orders restrained the soldier who first discovered the young rebel hanging from the oak. When Joab angrily demands why the trooper has not won a reward by killing the young upstart, the soldier replies: "Though I should receive a thousand pieces of silver, . . . yet would I not put forth my hand against the king's son." Old Joab shares no such scruples. What cares he for the king's command? Grasping three darts, he thrusts them through the heart of young Absalom. What an ignominious death for a handsome young prince who has set his heart on stealing his father's throne!

The body of the dead rebel is hurled into a near-by pit. Over it is heaped a pile of stones. His real monument, however, was to stand in Jerusalem. There he had erected a memorial pillar. Since he had no son to carry on the projected dynasty, the would-be king wished somehow to be remembered. So he has been widely recalled in every age, but always with execration. In history he has taken his place with other traitors, such as Cain and Haman, Judas and Benedict Arnold. Today in the Valley of Kedron, not far from where Judas betrayed our Lord, stands the so-called "Tomb of Absalom." In passing that way many a pious Jew stops to spit at the supposed resting place of Absalom. What an anticlimax for a would-be conqueror!

All this while the king has waited with baited breath. How will he receive the tidings about the battle in the woods? Will he give thanks because of victory, or will he bewail the fate of his boy? Is he first of all the king of Israel, or the father of Absalom? The answer comes out strongly in the account of the two messengers from the unseen battlefield. First of all, and most of all, David is a father!

3. *Two kinds of messengers* (vv. 19-32). The first courier to reach the king seems to have everything that heart can desire.

His assets include youth and the best of blue blood, with education and culture, as befits the son of the leading priest. This young Ahimaaz likewise shows a commendable desire to be useful. Skillfully he pleads his case for a chance to serve. He can easily outrun the other messenger to the king. The young courier must be endowed with personality and with every charm. He would commend himself to any congregation in quest of a pastor: "He is a good man, and cometh with good tidings." Who would not welcome such a young clergyman?

And yet young Ahimaaz fails, miserably. Why? Perhaps through lack of courage. When at length he arrives at the king's gate and begins to speak, the young messenger tells about the battle, but not about the son. Even after the impetuous father cries out, "Is it well with the young man Absalom?" the messenger dallies with the facts. He shows himself "too polite to tell the truth." He dare not utter what will cause pain. Hence he has to hear the fateful words "Turn aside!"

Thus the messenger of "sweetness and light" gives way to a nameless slave. "The Cushite" appears to be a Negro from Ethiopia. He has none of the other courier's gifts and graces. Devoid of youth and charm, education and culture, this lowly bearer of tidings has one asset: he can tell the truth. He can report facts as they took place. First he recounts the victory by the forces of righteousness. When the king asks about young Absalom, the messenger does not flinch. Indirectly, but unmistakably, he tells the truth. He might have served as one of the many object lessons in a book of popular addresses about "the marks of a man."[3] In speaking to college students the lecturer pointed to truth as the basic virtue in any man.

Pause to note the contrast. See the young messenger who does nothing with much, and the one who does much with nothing.

[3] Robert E. Speer, *The Marks of a Man* (Methodist Book Concern, 1907), pp. 15-46.

THE GRIEF OF A VICTORIOUS FATHER

When we church folk choose a herald, which one do we prefer? Do we elect the charming young fellow who sidesteps everything disagreeable, or the older one who does right at any cost? Sooner or later we shall hear our King say to the artful dodger: "Stand aside!" What a parable in action for everyone who dares to preach! But why do we linger so long with these side issues? Have we forgotten the sorrow of that grief-stricken father?

4. *The grief of a wartime father* (v. 33). "O my son Absalom, my son, my son Absalom! would I had died for thee, O Absalom, my son, my son!" This despairing cry from a father with a broken heart afforded the title for a recent best seller. Like more than a few books of late, this one borrowed its name from Holy Writ: *My Son, My Son!* [4]

This outcry from a father's heart might evoke a cruel response: "Old man, your grief and shame come far too late. Why did you not begin to live for your boy years ago? Why did you not set him an example of purity and honor?" But that is not the right way to deal with the Scriptures. Rather let every reader take the message home to his heart: "Lord, is it I?"

Especially let every young father review the scene in the spirit of prayer. Let him know that the most woeful tragedy on earth may be enacted in the bosom of a man who fails as a father. Then let him resolve that by God's grace he shall never have to shed such tears of remorse and shame. Why should not every father become a Christian for the sake of his boy?

[4] By Howard Spring, Viking, 1938.

CHAPTER 33

THE POWER OF A MAN'S PERSONALITY

II Samuel 23:15-17

HERE A BEAUTIFUL SCENE INVITES US TO STUDY DAVID'S PERSONALITY. For want of a better definition we may think of personality as the ability to lead others without resorting to force. We should also remember the countless variations of personality among gifted men. As one star differeth from another in glory, so did our king differ from everyone else on earth. Partly because he insisted on being himself, David became the most beloved character in Old Testament times. For the nonce we may ignore his grievous sins and think only about the secret of his charm. Nowhere do we come closer to the heart of the matter than when we hear him express a desire for a sip of water from the well back on the old home farm.

1. *A living example of personality.* When David longed for a sip of water from the well at Bethlehem, he showed the beauty of sentiment. According to a master of psychology, a sentiment means "a system of emotional tendencies organized round some object." [1] Such a way of looking at the facts would have bewildered King David. Like most other Hebrews, he did not excel in philosophy. He was not at all scientific. He felt more at home in the realm of feeling. He would have thought of a sentiment in terms of loyalty to what he loved, such as home or native land. He may not have been aware that such worthy feelings can go too far and degenerate into sickly sentimentality. That sort of effeminate weakness finds no place in the heart of a man like David.

[1] See Alexander F. Shand, *The Foundations of Character*, Macmillan, 1914.

THE POWER OF A MAN'S PERSONALITY

The chief sentiment of the king's heart seems to have been love for home. As a man grows older his thoughts turn more and more toward the place where his loved ones dwell. Even if they have gone away to their God, he cherishes recollections of the place where they used to dwell. From this angle look at the aging warrior out on his bivouac. Between the king and his boyhood home lie all the hosts of the Philistines. For what does his heart most yearn? For a sip of the water that he used to taste back in his home at Bethlehem. If this were all that we knew about David, we could infer that he had a heart full of sentiment.

Then too the king must have longed for peace. Throughout our Revolutionary War the heart of George Washington must often have journeyed far away across the hills to his beloved home at Mount Vernon. Would not every true warrior prefer to walk in the gentle paths of peace? That may be one of the many reasons why we honor the memory of Robert E. Lee. In our own times, also, many a stalwart warrior has done his duty, and vastly more, at the daily risk of his life. All the while he has longed for the hour when the cannon shall cease to roar. Then

> The only sound from its rusty throat
> Shall be a wren's or a bluebird's note,
> And nations shall learn war no more.

When David expressed a desire for a sip of water from the old home well, he afforded three of his followers an opportunity to show their loyalty. Loyalty means "the willing and practical and thoroughgoing devotion of a person to a cause," [2] as that cause is embodied in a leader. Those three lieutenants of David may not have been clear about the cause, but still they hazarded their lives for the king. As soon as they heard him speak about water, off they went to make their plans. They did not wait for his

[2] Josiah Royce, *The Philosophy of Loyalty* (Macmillan, 1908), p. 17; see also pp. 3-48.

command. That they knew would never come. They did not even tarry to consider the wisdom or the folly of what they were about to do. When has loyalty ever paused to count the cost?

Devotion to a leader calls for both courage and caution. If those three men had gathered about them three hundred others, the Gideon's band might have been wiped out. If the three had sallied forth together, they might all have been slain. Hence they parted. Each of them stole out along a different pathway through the hills, where they must have felt entirely at home. Even if one or two should be killed or captured, still they felt sure that their hero would have his heart's desire. Who but a leader with a heart could have inspired such devotion?

To men of a certain type this sort of loyalty seems quixotic. So does the Christlike spirit that takes a brilliant musician and scholar down into the midst of Africa to "throw away his life" as a missionary doctor. One of the fascinating books about Albert Schweitzer tells of an exhausting day in the clinic at Lambaréné. In the evening, after the last patient had gone out of the crude dispensary, the missionary flung himself down on a bench and exclaimed: "What a fool I am, that I have tried to be doctor to such savages!" "Yes," murmured Joseph, his native assistant, "on earth you are a big fool, but not in heaven!" [3]

When those three troopers returned with water that they had secured at the risk of their lives, King David reverently poured it out on the ground. How quixotic! Yes, perhaps, though the heart has reasons that the head cannot know. Dearly did the king prize the devotion of those friends. Well did he know the perils through which they had passed. Never would he forget their proof of loyalty and love. How could he have failed to regard that water as holy unto the Lord? Indeed, he must have looked on it as a sacrament, a visible sign of invisible grace. That must have

[3] See John D. Regester, *Albert Schweitzer: The Man and His Work* (Abingdon-Cokesbury, 1931), p. 95.

been why he poured it on the ground, as an offering unto God.

Notice also the grace and tact with which the king acknowledged the priceless gift. A man without a heart would have upbraided them for imperiling their lives, and jeopardizing the cause. David might have told them sternly that he needed their living powers and not their dead bodies. But a man of the domineering type would never have won the allegiance of such warriors. When shall we discover that strong men prefer to follow a leader with a heart as well as a head? The man with a heart under control receives a kindness as graciously as he bestows a favor.

These words about the water from Bethlehem's well have won literary fame. A parallel case appears in what our Lord said about the woman who showed her loyalty by pouring ointment on One about to die.[4] That proof of a good woman's devotion to her Redeemer called forth sneers from Judas. In like manner today, the outgoing of a person's heart often seems to the worldling quixotic. Even so, how else can one exert the power of personality? How else can one be pleasing unto God?

2. *The man after God's own heart.* While we are thinking about the personality of King David, we may face a question that has puzzled countless readers of the Bible. Why should he have been called the man after God's own heart? Twice this tribute appears in the Scriptures, once in First Samuel and again in the preaching of Paul.[5] Why did the chief interpreter of our religion endorse the saying of the Hebrew annalist? Doubtless because of David's personality. In order to please God, a man must have largeness of heart. In a far different fashion the Apostle himself had this quality. Otherwise how could Paul ever have penned his wondrous hymn of love?[6]

---

[4] See Matt. 26:12-13.
[5] I Sam. 13:14; Acts 13:22.
[6] I Cor. 13; see also James Stalker, *The Preacher and His Models,* pp. 159-62.

Love appears to be the best thing about any good man or woman. Such a person loves God supremely, loves others largely, and loves self last. In much the same manner the heart of the shepherd goes out to his sheep. Hence David liked to be known as the shepherd king. The man after God's own heart loved his home and his fatherland. Still more did he love his Church and his Lord. In short, his career seems to have been largely the outpouring of his heart in the service of God and of men.

But what about those sins that King David committed when he had passed middle age? At his best this man loved goodness, truth, and honor. At his worst he departed from godliness as far as a mortal could go. Nevertheless, the main current of his life kept moving toward God and the advancement of the Kingdom. In like manner the Mississippi River broadens and deepens in its course toward the gulf. If in time of flood that mighty stream bursts its banks and carries destruction in its wake, still we think of the Mississippi as a force for good and not for evil. Without any attempt to condone David's sins, we can look on him as honored of God in preparing the way for the coming Redeemer. Let us keep our eyes on the main current of his career.

Indeed, we may derive comfort from the fact that God used and honored King David, the adulterer and murderer. In like manner our Lord blessed John Newton, the former slave trader. If our Master required a perfect record before He would use and bless any of us in His service, who could qualify? In all fairness, however, we ought to remember that both King David and John Newton repented, and that each of them devoted the rest of his days to holy living.[7] The man after God's own heart may have shown himself weak and sinful. For that very reason he has learned to rely on the tender mercies of his God.

[7] More than one radio preacher in New York City makes capital of John Newton's composing hymns while engaged in the slave traffic. A reading of his biography, however, shows that a span of years separated the hymn writing from the slave selling. Meantime his life had been transformed.

THE POWER OF A MAN'S PERSONALITY

This truth about King David ought to bring solace and cheer to every man called of God to become a religious leader. The work demands reliance on God and greatness of heart. If leadership required the brilliancy of a genius or the excellencies of a saint, how many of us could qualify? But if the Lord simply asks the whole of a person, just as he stands, who can hesitate? God alone can summon any of us to become a leader. He can endow anyone with the needful gifts and graces. Indeed, He can "strike a mighty blow with a crooked stick."

Better still, our God can pardon and restore. He can permit such a sinner as David to become the progenitor of the Messiah. The best thing about our God must be His grace. In its upper reaches this means divine favor for the unworthy. On these terms any of us can qualify. Whatever your record in the past, why not become known as a man of God's own choosing?

CHAPTER 34

THE CAREER OF GOD'S CHOSEN LEADER

*II Samuel 24:24*b

"Neither will I offer burnt-offerings unto the lord my god which cost me nothing." Near the end of his career the king uttered these words, which might have served him as a lifelong motto. Whatever he undertook he carried out with all his might. In peace as in war, in public worship as in private sin, he threw into the deed of the moment all his God-given powers. When such a spirit seems sincere, as it always did with him, it quickly becomes contagious, if not irresistible. From this viewpoint let us endeavor to catch a bird's-eye view of David's career.

Chronologically, his life and work fall into three stages. The period of preparation included about thirty years.[1] The period of achievement lasted approximately twenty. The period of disappointment covered another score of years. Each of those stages had more or less to do with the shepherd king, and far more with the sovereignty of God.

1. *The Lord's training of the Shepherd King.* David's first thirty years constituted the period of preparation for future service. The same length of time appears in the records about Joseph in Egypt and about the Man of Galilee. A like period marked the early career of Albert Schweitzer and of many another who has made ready to serve in one of the learned professions. Who has ever found a quick and easy way to prepare for a career of usefulness? How then did the Lord God make young David ready for his career of achievement?

[1] In Hebrew history no such figures can be exact.

Providentially, the young man's heredity seems to have been excellent. His environment was that of a country lad remote from what we call civilization. The home life with Jesse on the sheep "ranch" at Bethlehem afforded endless opportunities for work as well as worship. The education of the future king must have been practical rather than scholastic. In American history both Washington and Lincoln became strong leaders without having learned much at school. Out among his sheep young David developed the powers that he later employed as a leader of men.

A good shepherd must serve as the leader and defender of his flock. Especially amid such hills as those around Bethlehem he must be courageous and resourceful. How else can he cope with wild beasts and human marauders? At times the work of the shepherd involves peril. More often it affords long hours of inactivity. Then a lad is able to study the stars or else enjoy music. If he will have it so, his long night vigils may bring him close to the heart of God. Thus it seems to have been with David, as it had formerly been with Moses. Out in the vast open spaces each of them discovered the nearness and the majesty of his God.

In early manhood David enjoyed the friendship of the crown prince. What such an experience can mean to a lad from the farm, who can know except one who has had a friend like Jonathan? As for advantages known as cultural, David enjoyed practically nothing, except in poetry and music. There he appears to have been self-taught. Even so, he became a master. Indeed, he stands out in history as perhaps the strongest and the most versatile of self-made men. But David himself would have ascribed all the glory to his God.

2. *The Lord's blessing on the Shepherd King.* The period of constructive achievement appears to have included only about twenty years. If so, what leader of men has ever accomplished so much in the face of obstacles apparently insurmountable? In order to appreciate what he did in upbuilding and stabilizing the

kingdom, read First Samuel and then turn to First Kings. Note the advancement during the period covered by Second Samuel. Remember that this man's reign prepared for Israel's "Golden Age." What other ruler ever did so much with so little, and that in only twenty years? What then did he accomplish?

The Shepherd King led his people in war. Despite the superior numbers and equipment of the foe, he won most of his battles and all of his campaigns. In time he drove out the invaders. Better still, he inspired the people to build up the nation. By his enthusiasm and his tact he induced the twelve divergent and clashing tribes to become a single united people. He guided them in selecting a new capital and in setting apart a central place for the worship of God. According to Hebrew tradition, which there is little reason to question, he became responsible for many of the psalms and for much of the other music in public worship. Whether he did the work himself, or inspired others to do it, King David must have become the prime mover in promoting beautiful worship. What a builder, both in State and in Church!

3. *The Lord's chastening of the Shepherd King.* At the age of fifty, alas, David seems to have grown weary of trying to be good. For a season he ceased to regard himself as the shepherd of the people. Up to that time he had set them an example of serving God amid an active career. All at once he fell into the grossest sins. From that time onward his years on earth were shadowed by sorrow. In a sense the calamities came as the judgment of God; from a different viewpoint his sorrows were self-imposed.

In his own family David kept reaping a harvest of woes. What he had done to another home and to the nation, his own children did to him and to his household. Why should they not follow in the footsteps of their father? Since he had been guilty of adultery, murder, and disloyalty to the nation, he should have been prepared to see his children do likewise. Soon the contagion of evil spread throughout the land. After the king stooped to the vilest forms of sin, more than one would-be usurper strove to seize the throne. In brief, when has a good man ever fallen farther? When has any "saint" ever suffered more tragically from the sins of his past?

Worst of all must have been the sorrows within David's soul. Throughout those last twenty years of anticlimax in his career, that pitiful king had to live with himself and his memories. His grief must have reached its lowest depths with the death of Prince Absalom as a traitor to the fatherland. At such a time how could the king forget the heights from which he had fallen, and the depths into which he had dragged his sons as weil as his subjects? On the contrary, how could he ever cease to give thanks for God's redeeming grace? Over against such a background read again the Fifty-first and the Thirty-second Psalm. Whether or not we look upon David as the author, those two songs show us the way to escape from despair because of sin. They also teach us to give thanks for the Shepherd King.

Before we say adieu to our three men in the books of Samuel, let us face the most astounding fact revealed in our study: Despite his shortcomings and his sins, David appears to have been the best of the kings in Judah or Israel. As such he became the progenitor of the Messiah. Concerning David the prophets wrote many of their most wondrous words about the coming Redeemer. Listen to a few of their messianic predictions:

Of the increase of his government and peace there shall be no end, upon the throne of David and upon his kingdom, to order it, and to establish it with judgment and with justice from henceforth even for ever.[2]

There shall come forth a rod out of the stem of Jesse, and a Branch shall grow out of his roots: and the spirit of the Lord shall rest upon him.[3]

[2] Isa. 9:7 (A.V.).
[3] Isa. 11:1-2a (A.V.).

I have found David the son of Jesse, a man after mine own heart, which shall fulfill all my will. Of this man's seed hath God according to his promise raised unto Israel a Saviour, Jesus.[4]

What weak and sinful human stuff our God can use in building up His Kingdom on earth! That must have been why the King of the Prophets wrote about the coming Messiah: "He shall grow up before him [the Lord God] as a tender plant, and as a root out of a dry ground."[5] If the Lord could bring the Saviour of the world out from the stock of David, the very same God surely can use the weakest and the worst of us.

In our dark days of rebuilding what war has thrown down, to whom shall the Church and the State look for leadership? To men like Samuel and David, but not to those like King Saul. Beyond and above even the best of human leaders let us behold our God. Then we can make our own the words that Winston Churchill quoted over the radio in one of the blackest hours of World War II:

> Say not the struggle nought availeth,
>   The labor and the wounds are vain,
> The enemy faints not, nor faileth,
>   And as things have been they remain.
>
> For while the tired waves, vainly breaking,
>   Seem here no painful inch to gain,
> Far back, through creeks and inlets making,
>   Comes silent, flooding in, the main
>
> And not by eastern windows only,
>   When daylight comes, comes in the light;
> In front, the sun climbs slow, how slowly,
>   But westward, look, the land is bright![6]

[4] Acts 13:22b-23 (A.V.).
[5] Isa. 53:2a (A.V.).
[6] Arthur Hugh Clough, *Poems* (Macmillan, 1903), p. 452.

242

BOOKS FOR FURTHER STUDY

*The Abingdon Bible Commentary, ed. Frederick C. Eiselen and others. New York and Nashville: Abingdon-Cokesbury Press, 1929.

Alexander, James W. Thoughts on Preaching. New York: Charles Scribner's Sons, 1861. "Expository Preaching," pp. 272-313.

Bewer, Julius A. The Literature of the Old Testament. New York: Columbia University Press, 1933.

*Blackwood, Andrew W. Preaching from the Bible. New York and Nashville: Abingdon-Cokesbury Press, 1941. "The Expository Lecture," chap. vii.

Blaikie, W. Garden. The Expositor's Bible. New York: A. C. Armstrong & Son, ca. 1888.

Broadus, John A. On the Preparation and Delivery of Sermons, new and rev. ed., ed. Jesse B. Weatherspoon. New York: Harper & Bros., 1944. Pp. 141-56.

Brown, Charles R. The Social Message of the Modern Pulpit (based on Exodus). New York: Charles Scribner's Sons, 1912.

Cadbury, Henry J. National Ideals in the Old Testament. New York: Charles Scribner's Sons, 1920.

Cartledge, Samuel A. A Conservative Introduction to the Old Testament. Athens, Ga.: University of Georgia Press, 1944.

*Davidson, Andrew B. The Called of God (sermonic addresses). Edinburgh: T. & T. Clark, 1903. "Saul's Reprobation," pp. 141-61.

Davis, John D. The Westminster Dictionary of the Bible, rev. and rewritten by Henry S. Gehman. Philadelphia: Presbyterian Board, 1944.

*Dods, Marcus. Israel's Iron Age, Sketches from the Period of the Judges. New York: Doubleday, Doran & Co., n.d.

*Driver, Samuel R. Notes on the Hebrew Text of Samuel. New York: Oxford University Press, 1913.

Eiselen, Frederick C. The Prophetic Books of the Old Testament.

* Books recommended for the initial study.

New York: The Methodist Book Concern, 1923. "The Books of Samuel," I, 63-86.

Erdmann, C. F. D. *Lange's Commentary,* tr. C. H. Toy and J. A. Broadus. New York: Charles Scribner's Sons, 1877.

Fosdick, Harry E. *The Modern Use of the Bible.* New York: The Macmillan Co., 1924.

Garstang, John. *The Heritage of Solomon.* London, 1924. "Nation and Kingship," chap. ix.

Gray, George B. *Sacrifice in the Old Testament.* New York: Oxford University Press, 1925.

Jeffs, Harry. *The Art of Exposition.* London, 1910.

*Keil, C. F., and Delitzsch, F. *Biblical Commentary on the Books of Samuel,* tr. James Martin. Edinburgh, 1886.

*Kennedy, Archibald R. S. *The New Century Bible.* New York: Frowde, 1905.

*Kirkpatrick, A. F. *The Cambridge Bible for Schools and Colleges.* London: Cambridge University Press, 1880-81.

*Knott, Harold E. *How to Prepare an Expository Sermon.* Cincinnati: Standard Publishing Co., 1930.

Macgregor, G. H. C. *Messages of the Old Testament, Genesis to Joel and Chronicles.* London, 1901.

Maclaren, Alexander. *Expositions of Holy Scripture.* New York: A. C. Armstrong & Son, 1907.

Meyer, Frederick B. *Expository Preaching, Plans and Methods.* New York: Doubleday, Doran & Co., 1912.

Morgan, G. Campbell. *The Ministry of the Word.* New York: Fleming H. Revell Co., 1919.

Oesterley, W. O. E., and Robinson, T. H. *A History of Israel.* New York: Oxford University Press, 1932.

Patton, Carl S. *The Use of the Bible in Preaching.* Chicago: Willett, Clark & Co., 1936.

Pfeiffer, Robert H. *Introduction to the Old Testament.* New York: Harper & Bros., 1941.

*Price, Ira M. *The Dramatic Story of Old Testament History.* New York: Fleming H. Revell Co., 1935.

BOOKS FOR FURTHER STUDY

Smith, George Adam. *Modern Criticism and the Preaching of the Old Testament.* New York: A. C. Armstrong & Son, 1901.

————. *The Historical Geography of the Holy Land,* rev. ed. New York: Harper & Bros., 1932.

Smith, Henry P. *The International Critical Commentary.* New York: Charles Scribner's Sons, 1899. (Technical.)

Taylor, William M. *The Ministry of the Word.* New York: Randolph & Sons, 1878. "Expository Preaching," pp. 155-67.

The Westminster Historical Atlas to the Bible, ed. G. E. Wright and F. V. Filson. Philadelphia: The Westminster Press, 1945.

Willett, Herbert L. *Studies in the First Book of Samuel.* Chicago: University of Chicago Press, 1909. (Elementary.)

ACKNOWLEDGMENTS

The following have kindly granted permission to quote selections from books subject to their copyright:

ABINGDON-COKESBURY PRESS for excerpt from *I Was Made a Minister*, by Bishop Edwin H. Hughes.

BOBBS-MERRILL COMPANY for excerpt from *Here We Are Again; Recollections of an Old Circus Clown*, by Robert E. Sherwood, copyright 1926. Used by special permission of the publishers.

T. & T. CLARK, Edinburgh, for excerpts from *The Called of God*, by A. B. Davidson.

DODD, MEAD & COMPANY for excerpt from *John Burnet of Barns*, by John Buchan.

E. P. DUTTON & COMPANY, New York, for excerpts from *Sermons*, by Phillips Brooks.

HARPER & BROTHERS for excerpts from *Introduction to the Old Testament*, by Robert H. Pfeiffer; and *Walkin' Preacher of the Ozarks*, by Guy Howard.

HOUGHTON, MIFFLIN COMPANY for excerpt from *Through Man to God*, by George A. Gordon.

THE INTERNATIONAL COUNCIL OF RELIGIOUS EDUCATION for quotations from the American Standard Version of the Revised Bible, copyright 1929.

THE MACMILLAN COMPANY for excerpts from *A Dictionary of Religion and Ethics*, ed. Shailer Mathews and G. B. Smith; *The Rise of Christian Education*, by Lewis J. Sherrill; *The English Bible as a Guide to Writing*, by Charles S. Baldwin; and "Say Not the Struggle," from *Poems*, by Arthur Hugh Clough.

CHARLES SCRIBNER'S SONS for excerpt from *The Servant of the Word*, by Henry H. Farmer.

WILSON, MRS. WOODROW, for excerpts from an address by Woodrow Wilson at McCormick Theological Seminary.

INDEX

INDEX

[Italic figures refer to chapters, roman figures to pages]

INDEX

251

[Italic figures refer to chapters, roman figures to pages]

INDEX

[Italic figures refer to chapters, roman figures to pages]

INDEX

255

[Italic figures refer to chapters, roman figures to pages]